Decoding the Enigma of *"NATURAL MAN"* in Mark Twain's Works

TARO MAEYASHIKI

INDIA · SINGAPORE · MALAYSIA

CONTENTS

MARK TWAIN'S BIOGRAPHY

Mark Twain (1895)

Illustration by Napoleon Sarony

(in Public Domain)

Samuel Langhorne Clemens (Clemens adopted the pen name Mark Twain at age 28) was born on November 30, 1835, in the village of Florida, Missouri, and moved to Hannibal, Missouri, at the age of four. Twain attended school for only a short time because of the sudden death of his father in 1847. When his father died, Twain was only 11 years old.

For a time, he worked as a delivery and office boy, and by the age of 15, he began writing articles under various pseudonyms. His first article, "A Gallant Fireman," appeared in the *Western Union*, Hannibal's newspaper run by his brother Orion; by age 17, Twain had become critical of the "Democratic governor and legislature," and in 1852, he wrote a satirical article in the *Hannibal Journal* entitled "Blabbing Government Secrets!" (Konstam 8).

Wanting to realize his dream of a successful career and wealth, Twain left home in 1853 and went to St. Louis, hoping to visit more eastern cities and turn his fortunes around. Meanwhile, he wrote to Orion, explaining that he would return to see his mother and his elderly sister Pamela only after he had become wealthy (Kamei 205).

In 1857, intrigued by information about coca in South America, Twain set out by steamboat for South America in search of fortune (Loving 44). On his way, at his first stop in New Orleans, he met Horace Bixby, a Mississippi River boat pilot who had been in the business for many years, but had never been to South America. After speaking with Bixby, Twain became interested in the Mississippi pilotage business. He asked Bixby to offer him an apprenticeship opportunity on the condition that he pay $500 for tuition. Bixby agreed to help him, and Twain set out to become a Mississippi steamboat pilot.

While learning the skills necessary to sail between St. Louis and New Orleans, Twain embraced the "sublime nature" of the Mississippi (Kamei 420). He was licensed as a pilot in 1859 and made a living in his profession until the Civil War broke out.

Unfortunately, Twain's satisfaction with riverboat pilotage was suddenly diminished by the death of his brother, Henry Clemens. Twain was, at the time, the pilot of the steamboat *Pennsylvania* and had worked for Henry as a clerk on that steamboat (Dempsey 252). Due to mechanical problems, *Pennsylvania*'s boiler exploded, and Henry was killed. Emerson observes that this catastrophe led Twain to a "deterministic philosophy" (Emerson 10). Struggling with guilt over his brother's death, Twain developed a personal philosophy that tragedy was not a personal responsibility but rather a twist of fate.

In 1861, the outbreak of the Civil War ended Twain's work as a pilot. Shortly after the outbreak of the Civil War, United States President Abraham Lincoln appointed his brother Orion as the new Secretary of the Territory of Nevada (Youngblood 38). During this period, Clemens wrote *Roughing It*, "an account of his travels and adventures in Nevada, California, and Hawaii between 1861 and 1866 (Railton 18).

With the perfect opportunity to explore the West, he hoped to find Native Americans, as described by Fenimore Cooper. Those Twain encountered were the tribe he calls the fictional "Goshoot Indians" in Chapter 19 of *Roughing It*, an intentional misspelling of the Goshute tribe that occupied what is now western Utah and eastern Nevada.

While exploring the West, Twain also became interested in silver mining. He attempted to prospect as far as the town of Aurora, Nevada, but could not find any silver and subsequently lost all the money he had invested in mining stocks. Bankrupt, he was forced to continue his work as a newspaper reporter, writing articles containing hoax elements and captured people's attention with his unique sense of humor (Kamei 421).

In 1863, Twain began to write under the pen name "Mark Twain." This slang term from riverboats indicates a depth of about 3.7 meters, the depth of water at which a steamboat can safely navigate. He used this term as a pseudonym from that time on. This decision to use the pilotage term from the Mississippi to express his identity as a writer reveals a peculiarity of his character.

Twain left Nevada for San Francisco and began writing news stories in 1864 while working as a *San Francisco Morning Call* reporter. There, inspired by Jim Gillis's humorist skills, Twain came to appreciate the value of real stories (Kamei 422).

Around this time, Twain also began to express a critical attitude toward "world authorities" and "snobs who value genteel tradition" (Izuka 65). Later, Twain was 40 years old when, at the celebration of John Greenleaf Whittier's 70th birthday, he performed a burlesque in front of them that poked fun at such famous East Coast writers as Ralph Waldo Emerson, Henry Wadsworth Longfellow, and Oliver Wendell Holmes. He had a critical attitude toward these established writers, and his snobbish mannerisms are evident (Kamei 34).

At the age of 29, Twain wrote a short story, "The Celebrated Jumping Frog of Calaveras County" (1865), while trying to master the art of literary hoaxing. The story was based on "The Jumping Frog" by Ben Kuhn. The various comical elements in this tale are clearly linked.

While gaining fame as a storyteller, Twain began to demonstrate other talents apart from writing: in 1867, he was given the opportunity to give a speech in New York. He soon became known as a phenomenal orator, able to attract and entertain large audiences regardless of nationality or creed. He soon became known as a phenomenal orator, able to attract and entertain large audiences regardless of nationality or creed.

While engaged in this work, Twain had the opportunity to participate in an excursion to Europe and the Holy Land on the steamship *Quaker City*, on which he met fellow passenger Charles Langdon. His book *The Innocents Abroad* (1869) is based on this experience. After he visited Palestine, he became convinced that the Bible was nothing more than a "myth" (Emerson 66).

Later, Twain visited the Langdon residence. The Langdons were wealthy but modest and mild-mannered. They had been strong proponents of abolishing slavery. They helped slaves escape their masters via the "Underground Railroad" and even had the opportunity to help a notable African American leader, Frederick Douglass. The Langdon family minister was Thomas Beecher, brother of prominent abolitionist Harriet Beecher Stowe (Emerson 55-56).

At the Langdon home, Twain met Charles Langdon's sister, Olivia Langdon, and fell in love at first sight. Twain asked Olivia to be his wife, but she refused.

This was because she was "the genteel girl of the Victorian era" and Twain was a "wild humorist of the Pacific Slope (Meltzer 123)." He stopped smoking and drinking and tried to become a real Christian. Eventually, the family embraced this Western man. Twain and Olivia were finally married in 1870.

Twain played the role of a serious Christian during his courtship with Olivia, but his skepticism was only heightened by his Quaker City experience. Emerson notes that "Clemens's skepticism about traditional Christianity" had begun to manifest itself while they were in San Francisco (Emerson 163). When Twain's temporary enthusiasm for religious observances cooled, Olivia followed his lead (Emerson 66-67). Twain's skepticism was not only a result of his Quaker City experience but also of his own experience with the Quakers.

Their life together after marriage was both happy and miserable. First came the misfortune of Olivia's father dying of cancer within a year. Three months later, Twain's first and only son, Langdon Clemens, was born, but he died of diphtheria in 1872. However, married life was not all darkness. Later that same year, Twain's oldest daughter, Susy Clemens, was born.

In 1868, Twain met and befriended Joseph Twichell, the pastor of the Congregationalist Church in Hartford, Connecticut. Their friendship lasted more than 40 years until Twain's death.

Around 1869, the clergyman had begun to express his criticism of "political corruption," especially the "machine politics" of the Democratic Party, which he believed to be at the root of countless social problems and "poverty" in New York (Emerson 50). Twain and Twichell's continuing relationship illustrated his growing frustration with various aspects of American society.

In 1868, Twain began writing a short story, "Captain Stormfield's Visit to Heaven". Because Stormfield is "frank, forthright, irrepressible, authentic-though at times fooled by his own expectations," he is a character not unlike Twain himself (Emerson 127).

In 1873, Twain and co-author Charles Dudley Warner published *The Gilded Age*. The book satirized corrupt government officials by discussing the frenzied financial activities of public officials during the California gold rush (1848-1855). The book was the first to embody Twain's newfound antipathy toward American politicians.

The term "Gilded Age" is still used today to describe that period in American history.

Needless to say, Twain's career as a writer was successful at this point, and his good fortune was further enhanced by the birth of his second daughter, Clara Clemens, in 1874. With his growing family, Twain built a mansion in Hartford, Connecticut. His future seemed bright.

One of Twain's best-known works, *The Adventures of Tom Sawyer*, was written during this period and published in 1876. Not only are the various antics of Tom and his friends comically depicted, but it also involves a murder by a Native American called "Injun Joe." Injun Joe disappears from town after Tom reports that he witnessed the murder. Even though Tom and Huck fear that Injun Joe may show up and come after them, they do not retreat to their home and relax in relative safety. By chance, they encounter Injun Joe and friends discussing plans to bury the stolen treasure. At the end of the story, Tom and Huck discover a treasure worth $12,000 and become the town's heroes for their exploits.

In 1880, Twain's third daughter, Jean Clemens, was born. Starting in the same year, Twain invested $200,000 in the development of the prototype Paige typesetting machine. In 1881, Twain's book *The Prince and the Pauper* was published.

In this tale, the prince and the poor commoner decide to use their identical appearances to swap positions and explore worlds and experiences previously unknown to them.

While embracing life on the East Coast, Twain reminisced about his former life on the Mississippi. In 1883, he published his autobiographical memoir, *Life on the Mississippi*, in which he recalled his experiences as a riverboat pilot and his impressions of the Mississippi River.

In 1884, Twain's most famous work, *Adventures of Huckleberry Finn*, was published. In this novel, Huck, a boy of about 14, and his friend Jim, a fugitive slave, attempt to escape from St. Petersburg, Missouri, where they had been living, and travel upriver to Illinois, a free state. Unfortunately, the great current of the Mississippi causes them to head in the opposite direction, downstream to the Deep South. After Jim is captured and taken in by Tom Sawyer's relatives, Tom and Huck attempt to rescue him, but Tom is shot in the leg and is unable to continue his journey. For his part in saving Tom, Jim is exonerated and set free.

Adventures of Huckleberry Finn became a bestseller; however, because of its straightforward treatment of issues such as slavery and racism, some libraries, including the Concord Library in Massachusetts, refused to hold the book.

He received an honorary master's degree in literature from Yale University in 1888.

After writing *Adventures of Huckleberry Finn*, Twain began writing *Huck Finn and Tom Sawyer Among the Indians*, a sequel to *Adventures of Huckleberry Finn*. In this book, Tom, Huck, and Jim decide to travel to Indian Territory in search of adventure. At first, they meet a seemingly generous and peaceful tribe, but soon, the Native Americans become violent and kill a white family the boys meet on their journey.

Following his greatest successes, *Life on the Mississippi* and *Adventures of Huckleberry Finn*, Twain wrote *A Connecticut Yankee in King Arthur's Court* (1889) and *Pudd'nhead Wilson* (1894). These two stories are closely related to his view of the post-Reconstruction South. Both implicitly satirize various issues related to slavery. *A Connecticut Yankee in King Arthur's Court* has also been characterized as showing certain feudal aspects of 19th-century American democracy. For example, Emerson sees the book as satirizing the Catholic Church's vicious attempts to thwart "human freedom and progress" (Emerson 211).

Twain's literary life was going well until 1890, when his mother, Jane Clemens, drowned in a bathtub because of a seizure. Moreover, within the next six years, Twain's daughter Susy died of meningitis.

These incidents were only the beginning of the tragedies that the Clemens family would eventually face. The failure of the Paige Compositor and losses at his ailing publishing house, which would go bankrupt in 1894, found him $160,000 in debt. Suddenly short of money, Twain decided to go and live in Europe with his family to take advantage of the favorable exchange rates of the time. Fortunately for Twain, Henry Huttleston Rogers, an executive at Standard Oil, helped him out of his financial difficulties. He gave Twain important financial advice and even negotiated with his creditors (Kamei 301). Twain decided to go on another speaking tour with his family to earn money.

His speaking abilities were highly regarded, and he was probably confident that he would be able to pay off some of his debts with speaking fees. On this trip, Twain visited various countries, including Canada, India,

Australia, New Zealand, and South Africa, where he spoke incessantly (*The Mark Twain Encyclopedia,* xvi).

Thus, in a short time, Twain experienced the ordeal of losing the fortune he had dreamed of and struggling to get out of debt.

While traveling around Australia for lectures, Twain learned about the history and culture of various ethnic groups. Hearing of the harsh conditions faced by the aborigines, he became increasingly antagonistic toward imperialism. According to John Carlos Rowe, Twain took a stand against the U.S. colonization of the Philippines. He also criticized the annexation of the Congo Free State by King Leopold II of Belgium and the exploitation of Russians, Poles, and Finns by Tsar Nicholas II of Russia and published several anti-imperialist essays, including "To the Person Sitting in Darkness" (1901), *King Leopold's Soliloquy* (1905), and "The Czar's Soliloquy" (1905) (Rowe 122).

In *The Chronicles of Young Satan* (written between 1897 and 1900), Twain deals with the pettiness of corrupt human life and the sins of civilization. The protagonists of the story are the narrator, Theodor Fischer, and his friends Nikolaus Baumann and Seppi Wohlmeyer. They meet Young Satan in the form of a boy. The boy uses magic to entertain them.

In 1906, Twain wrote a short story titled "What is Man?" This story depicts an individual who is controlled not by the individual's free will but by the environment.

In 1902, Twain returned to his hometown of Hannibal to visit his parents' graves. This visit to Hannibal was to be his last. In 1909, Twain wrote the story *Letters from the Earth,* which depicts Satan's rebuke of the Christian God for his egoistic experiments on humans and animals through letters to the archangels Michael and Gabriel.

On April 21, 1910, Twain died at the age of 74, suffering from "physical ailments (Emerson 182)." In addition to the aforementioned honorary Master of Arts degree from Yale University, Twain also received a Doctor of Law degree from Oxford University in 1907. He lost many loved ones but was survived by his second daughter, Clara Clemens, who lived until 1962. He never gave up his adventurous way of life and continued to write passionately until his death.

INTRODUCTION

Ernest Miller Hemingway (1899-1961) praised Mark Twain by saying: "All modern American literature comes from one book by Mark Twain called Huckleberry Finn (Hemingway 261)." While William Faulkner (1897-1962), in an interview during his visit to Japan in 1955, described Twain as "the first truly American writer" (Zuckert 155). [1]

Twain wrote more than 30 books and more than 60 short stories. Each work deals with "social problems and prejudices," "gender, minorities," and ethical issues such as "moral corruption," which may surprise the reader. Twain's sensational works, such as *Adventures of Huckleberry Finn*, which dealt with the issue of slavery, were highly praised as masterpieces, but some states in the U.S. banned them from being used as school textbooks. For example, it was banned in New York, Philadelphia, and the Massachusetts town of Concord. There are many possible interpretations for understanding Twain's controversial works.

Twain's collected works have attracted much attention in Japan, and since 2002, the Japan Mark Twain Society has published a journal with an annual theme. The society has published 22 volumes of Japanese-language issues and six volumes of English-language issues, making it the only Twain Society in Japan with a proven track record.

The first issue of the *Journal of Mark Twain Studies*, "Mark Twain and the Logic of Techno-Views" (2002), discussed how Twain, who lived through the "technological age" of the "energy revolution" (9) and "technological revolution" (9), created his works from the perspective

---

[1] Faulkner did not record what he said in the interview at this time in his autobiography or writings, and what he said in this interview was recorded during his visit to Japan.

of science (9). According to Naohisa Tomita, the episode of *No. 44, The Mysterious Stranger* shows Twain's growing interest in "cinema" (38). In another review, Naoto Sugiyama argues that Twain found his "place" not in "a northern town that was being modernized with the help of technology" (61) but in "an unnamed rural southern town that disappeared with the flow of the Mississippi River" (61).

In the second issue of the *Journal of Mark Twain Studies*, "Mark Twain and the Detective Novel" (2003), Yoko Tsujimoto said that Twain, like Edgar Allan Poe, wrote "detective novels that are considered canonical" (61), mixing "fresh novel techniques" (9) and "social criticism" (9) with humor, and added parody, thereby clearly indicating "the limits of detective fiction" (61). Tsujimoto thinks that the inclusion of parody obscured the essence of the detective novel (61).

The third issue of the *Journal of Mark Twain Studies*, "Mark Twain and Fantasy" (2004), reconsidered whether Twain was a realist writer. The reason cited was that elements of fantasy in his novel *Adventures of Huckleberry Finn* can be found in several of his other works (9). Yoko Arima pointed out that the fantasy Twain depicted was "rational" (23) and close to "reality" (23). Akira Shibuya concluded that Twain's fantasies "contain human, accusatory content" (52-53).

The fourth issue of the *Journal of Mark Twain Studies*, "Mark Twain and Travel" (2005), shows that when Twain went to Asia, the Middle East, and Europe to lecture, he was influenced by local cultures in many ways. Masago Igawa, in reading Twain's travelog, suggests that when Twain visited India, Australia, and South Africa, "despite his contempt and criticism of the arrogance of white civilization, he regarded the 'blessings of civilization' for the uncivilized lands as unavoidable" (60). It has been noted that Twain's exposure to colonialism strengthened his stance as a social critic (60).

The fifth issue of the *Journal of Mark Twain Studies*, "Mark Twain and the Strangers" (2006), considered how Twain used his depiction of the socially vulnerable and the mysterious or indecipherable as strangers to criticize "the values of the American community" (9) and even conducted a self-analysis (9). Rie Egashira believes that Twain's break with the connection to the Mississippi River influenced his later works and contributed to the multiple appearances of characters in the roles of "destroyer" (25) and "rescuer" (25). Egashira argues that Twain faced reality and severed his relationship with the Mississippi to overcome his "deteriorating economic condition and the death of his family" (25). Ryo Waguri focuses on the strangers (38) and says that even though they are "reticent" (38), they satirize "the current state of American society and human society" and point out "the internal and spiritual problems of man" (38).

In the sixth issue of the *Journal of Mark Twain Studies*, "Huck Finn in Japan" (2007), Japanese Twain studies are reconsidered (9). Tsuyoshi Ishihara states that postwar Japanese have had more opportunities to read Twain's works as translated books. According to Ishihara, translators emphasized the image of Huck and Tom as heroes of democracy, trying to dispel negative images and idealize them (38). The actual images of Huck and Tom that Twain was trying to convey were temporarily sealed away (40).

In the seventh issue of the *Journal of Mark Twain Studies*, "Mark Twain and the South" (2008), the importance of the South's close involvement in Twain's literature was emphasized (9). Masago Igawa considered Hannibal, where Twain grew up, as "a society with slaves" (10), and by examining the "culture that tolerated slavery" (10), he asserted that Hannibal became the "mother of Twain's world of work" (21).

In the eighth issue of the *Journal of Mark Twain Studies*, "Mark Twain and Religion" (2009), discussed how Twain, who was said to be an "atheist" (9), was asked to reconsider his views on religion (9). Various religious experiences shaped Twain's complex religious views. According to Tetsuo Uenishi, Twain attended a Presbyterian church with his mother as a child, and his father was a member of the Freemasons (Uenishi 13-15). It seems that Twain often interacted with African American slaves of heretical beliefs that were close to him (14).

The ninth issue of the *Journal of Mark Twain Studies*, "Mark Twain and Capitalism" (2010), discussed Twain's work on *The Gilded Age,* co-authored with Charles Dudley Warner. Uzawa Yoshiko highlighted the issue of "political corruption" (12) in his work. The content of this work expresses a negative view of capitalism. However, the authors, Twain and Warner, intended to make a profit by making the book a bestseller (11).

In the tenth issue of the *Journal of Mark Twain Studies*, "The 100th Anniversary of Mark Twain's Death (International Forum) (2011)," the discussion of Twain's literature was conducted in terms of his contact with Faulkner, sexuality, morality, and comparisons with other writers. As an example, Tsuyoshi Ishihara pointed out that current literary history may be "a brilliant discussion that emphasizes only one aspect" (52). He offers the opinion that in order to determine "the essence of Twain" (53), it is essential to "cover the various aspects of Twain's life in a balanced manner, considering his turbulent life and the American movements of his time, while also paying attention to new and old critical movements."

The eleventh issue of the *Journal of Mark Twain Studies*, "American Literature and Autobiography" (2012), focused on Twain's dictated autobiography. Twain's autobiography is filled with humor, episodes about his family, and his feelings about minorities. Toshio Watanabe notes that Twain based his oral recordings on his memory; therefore, the authenticity of the recordings is uncertain (16). According to Watanabe, "In autobiography, it is important that the subject of the story and the object of the story are the same" (16), and he argues that "the past man who created the present man is also a fictional entity created by the memories or imagination of the past man who is writing his autobiography." (16)

In the twelfth issue of the *Journal of Mark Twain Studies*, "Mark Twain and Children" (2013), a discussion of Twain's peculiar and difficult-to-interpret child characters was presented (9). Kazuhiko Goto, from the perspective of similarities between Twain's characters, stated that Jim in *Adventures of Huckleberry Finn* and Hendon in *The Prince and the Pauper* share "an affection for Huck and Edward" (7) in terms of their "love for one boy" (7). Rie Egashira also discusses the "disguise" of children. As an example, Egashira points to the "problem of narration" (19) about Huck's dressing up as various characters, such as a little girl and "the boy who fell off the steamboat" (12), and his serving as narrator as well as character in the story (12-19), and she notes that with "Mark Twain and Huckleberry

Finn, both of which are Clemens' creations, the narrative problem is further extended." (19)

The thirteenth issue of the *Journal of Mark Twain Studies*, "Mark Twain and War" (2014), discussed Twain's views on war and his war-themed works in the context of the "Civil War" (9) and "War in the Early 20th Century" (9). Keiko Misugi discussed Dos Passos, with whom he shares a common critique of "imperialist war," and their "dislike and disappointment" in America (33). Also discussed was Twain's work *Personal Recollections of Joan of Arc*. At first glance, Ryo Waguri said, Twain seems to glorify Joan of Arc and emphasize her purity. However, Waguri says, "Joan is responsible for the deaths of many of her enemies and allies. This is a new way of looking at Twain's Joan." (44)

In the fourteenth issue of the *Journal of Mark Twain Studies*, "Dickens and Twain" (2015), Katsumi Satouchi states that Twain was influenced by Dickens' *American Notes for General Circulation* (1842) (29). According to Satouchi, both authors share "the same view of America and the way slavery is depicted in each work" (36). Miyuki Amano compares the two men's views on Native Americans and points out that "for Twain, Indians were an inseparable part of his life and a matter of his own identity" (64), compared to Dickens, who was able to maintain a spatial and psychological distance from Native Americans.

In the fifteenth issue of the *Journal of Mark Twain Studies*, "Twain and the West" (2016), the theme of "the West," rather than "the South," which has been the focus of attention in Twain's studies, was discussed (9). Since the "western" theme is similar to the "natural" theme addressed in this paper, we will introduce more previous studies. Takako Takeda states that: "In 1868, *The Adventures of Tom Sawyer was* published, and the pastoral depiction of the Midwest in this work contributed greatly to the representation of the West at that time" (14). Takeda also points out that Twain "had his own scheming involvement in the process of becoming known as a national icon, and that Twain, representing the American West, was incorporated into the process of the West being recognized as the American West at the same time" (17). Ryuzo Hamamoto, on the other hand, offers an interesting discussion of Twain's depiction of animals in the

West. Hamamoto comments that "Twain did not depict Western animals as they really were, but animals that projected his idea of 'Westernness' (28). As an example, he considers that "the story of the dumb blue jay projects a side of the illiterate but naive westerner" (28). According to Toru Kawamoto, the western stage was a place of "self-direction" for Twain (34). He believes that "Twain skillfully used the West as a brand image for himself as a writer and director of Westerns" (34), that his "vision" included "West and East, North and South," and he became widely known in America as "an artist of the American West" (35).

The American West reminds us of the untamed nature that existed before the disappearance of the frontier. The Native Americans, who also have a deep connection with nature, lived in the wilderness before white settlement. In this sense, "the West" and "nature" are closely linked.

In these studies by the Japanese Mark Twain Society, we can see that there are multiple discussions on the themes of "civilization" and "nature", such as "technology" in the first issue of the Society's journal.

Before examining previous studies on "civilization," I would like to describe some historical background that is essential for understanding Twain's works. Twain lived from the mid-19th century to the early 20th century, when the United States was expanding westward under the slogan "Manifest Destiny." In 1848, the U.S. government overcame Mexico and acquired territory in Texas, California, and other areas. At this time, the railroad network was developed, the East and West became more economically linked, and a gold rush occurred in California.

With this historical background in mind, we will introduce previous studies on "civilization" and Twain literature.

First, Chifuyu Fujii considers the American South a civilized society and describes it as follows:

Huck and Jim's attempt to escape civilized society in search of "freedom" is also seen in their rejection of the values and morals of American society at the time. (220)

Fujii shows that Huck's actions were in defiance of the values and morals of the time. David Tomlinson further elaborates on the era's moral and Christian views:

Huck befriends the runaway slave Jim. Jim wants to join his wife and family. Huck aids him in his plans to escape, not only defying community standards and national law but, as he understood it, God's law. (Tomlinson 121)

As can be seen from the above quote, Huck tried to help Jim, a fugitive slave, even though he knew that he was violating both the morality and the Christian discipline of the time.

In another study, Robert Bruce describes Huck's situation of escaping from civilized society as follows:

Under the abusive eye of Pap, Huck attempts to romanticize a life free from the intrusions of a judgmental society and constrictive civilization. Away from the enforced rules of school and town, Huck is "free" to exist [...]. (Bruce 89)

In other words, according to Bruce, the civilized society in *Adventures of Huckleberry Finn* is a repressive society that makes unilateral decisions and is rule-driven. Bruce also points out that by escaping the constraints of civilized society, Huck gains freedom.

Elsewhere, in *Adventures of Huckleberry Finn,* Keisuke Suzuki points out that Mrs. Watson and others educate and discipline Huck to "civilize" him and make him Christian (35).

In fact, Twain has a civilized side to him. What kind of people are "civilized people"? The following is a quote from Hirotsugu Inoue's definition of a "civilized person."

Civilized people live surrounded by luxury in the hope of an easy life, but they are also burdened with debts, and they live their whole lives without the simple, everyday comforts that savages enjoy [...]. (Inoue 45, cited and translated by Taro Maeyashiki)

The above quote applies to Twain's life: in 1861, Twain went to the Nevada Territory with Orion, who was appointed by the Lincoln government as Secretary of the Nevada Territory (Kamei 421), and in 1862, Twain tried to profit from a mining town called Aurora. This venture failed and he went bankrupt, but it is typical of civilized people to engage in this kind of speculative behavior. Also important is the following quote that illustrates Twain's financial ambitions.

> What drives Clemens [Mark Twain] above all else is his dream of success and his desire to be rich, which drives him from Hannibal to St. Louis and from St. Louis to the eastern cities until he is eighteen years old, when he writes to his brother Orion that he will not return to Missouri to see his mother's face or sister Pamela's face until he is rich." (Kamei 205, cited and translated by Taro Maeyashiki)

This dream of Twain would eventually come true: in 1870, Twain married Olivia, the daughter of a wealthy man, and they became multimillionaires. Once on the right track, Twain built a mansion in 1874 with $120,000 in capital and lived a wealthy life (Kamei 17). After investing $200,000 in the Paige typesetter between 1880 and 1894, he experienced bankruptcy again, partly because of the economic depression in 1893 (Kamei 38). As a result, he was $160,000 in debt, so Twain moved with his family to Europe to raise funds through lecture tours around the world (Kamei 38). He visited and lectured in Canada, India, Australia, New Zealand, South Africa, and other countries, completely paying off his debts (Kamei 38-39). Thus, Twain led a tumultuous life, experiencing both dreams and bankruptcy. It is certain that these experiences as a civilized man influenced Twain's work.

Next, we will look at previous studies on "nature." Twain's experience of nature is essential to understanding his works and is defined by the Mississippi River. In 1857, Twain wanted to go to South America to make a fortune, but he met Horace Bixby, a steamboat pilot on the Mississippi River, who interested him in the profession of pilotage and offered him an apprenticeship (Kamei 26). In 1859, he obtained his pilot's license and continued to work in the profession until the outbreak of the Civil War

(Kamei. 26). Works including *The Adventures of Tom Sawyer*, *Adventures of Huckleberry Finn*, and *Life on the Mississippi* are all based on the great river and the pen name he first adopted in 1863 was "a technical term he used when he was a pilot" before he began his career as a writer (Kamei 29).

The Mississippi has the most significant influence on Twain (26-27), but other influences include the nature of the countryside where Twain was born and raised. In his autobiography, he wrote exquisitely about the woods near his uncle's house from his childhood as follows:

> I can see the woods in their autumn dress, the oaks purple, the hickories washed with gold, the maples and the sumacs luminous with crimson fires, and I can hear the rustle made by fallen leaves as we plowed through them. I can see the blue clusters of wild grapes hanging among the foliage of the saplings, and I remember the taste of them and the smell. (*The Autobiography of Mark Twain* 16)

These descriptions show Twain's keen eye for observation.

The first major study on "nature" in Twain's writing is *The Mythic World of Huck and Tom* by Morio Sano. In *Adventures of Huckleberry Finn*, Sano explores "a narrative motif similar to the snake-slaying and dragon-slaying that frequently appear in world mythology" and discusses the work from the "perspective of snake-slaying" (Sano 219). Although not the author's purpose in this paper, Sano mentions the similarity between Rousseau's natural man and Huck multiple times which is important as a prior study of the "natural child-like Huck" in this paper. He states that the conditions to become a "natural child" are "independence" (13) and "wildness" (13). He states in Chapter 4 that Huck's "title of natural child" (13) ceases to be met when he begins to adjust to his new life with Widow Douglas. However, he states that Huck has not lost his "independence" and "wildness" as a natural child because of his new life, and that the "civilized element" (14) and the "natural child element" (14) "coexist" (14) or "conflict" (14) even after chapter 4. He wrote *The Mythic World of Huck and Tom* with the "conflict between nature and civilization" and "good and evil" in mind (219-220), but in his earlier opinion, the elements of both nature and civilization are in Huck. If this is the case, the author believes that civilization and nature are not in conflict. In this paper, too, nature and civilization are not seen as opposites but as overlapping. Sano further describes Huck as similar to Jean-Jacques Rousseau's savages, although there is no evidence of this. While this is extremely important as a precursor to this paper's view of the similarity between Twain's character and Rousseau's natural man, Sano's impression is limited to "they are similar." This paper differs from Sano's study in that it does not stop at this idea, but instead seeks to decipher the character's message from his perspective as a natural man while exploring the evidence for this similarity.

Major prior studies of the "natural child" are "Huckleberry Finn's America," "Huckleberry Finn is Now," and "Mark Twain's World," all written by Shunsuke Kamei. Kamei's argument centers on the conflict between nature and civilization, with Huck as the main character. In "Huckleberry Finn's America," Kamei sees the protagonist Huck as a "natural child" (4) who is "outside the social order" (5) in his quest for freedom. In his take on "nature," Kamei emphasizes the Garden of Eden-esque nature (10). Kamei describes Huck as "a boy who lives independently and is not bound by the heavy social order, but lives freely" (7). Kamei also describes Huck as an "American Adam" (12). Corinna Siebert Ruth also describes the connection between Huck and the natural world as follows:

> In the journey down the river, we see Huck's movement away from civilization, with its corrupt institutions, and toward the natural world of the river. Here Huck's feeling for the natural beauty of the river gives the novel a mythological characteristic. (Ruth 36)

In other words, Huck, fleeing a corrupt and civilized society, is fascinated by the beauty of the Mississippi, and it is this inspiration that gives the novel its mystical element.

According to Yukiko Asahi, "nature" in Mark Twain's literature refers to the Mississippi River. He explains that the river has constantly influenced Twain since his childhood and is significant from a global and historical perspective (70).

Seiji Honjo also cites the "Mississippi River" (55), the setting of *Adventures of Huckleberry Finn,* "Jackson Island," "the woods near the town of St. Petersburg," and "an Indian tribe" (55) as examples of nature. Honjo defines nature as "something natural, unmanipulated, and unartificial" (55), and says that as industry has developed, people have lost sight of the value of nature's existence (55). He notes Huck's keen senses and his depiction of nature (56). He also contrasts "life in the forest" with "the Douglas family" as "wild life" and "enculturated order and discipline" (57), and notes the contrast between nature and civilization as follows:

> Twain's aim seems to be to appreciate the innocent way of life of a natural child like Huck, and at the same time, in contrast to the real world, to appeal to the reader by cleverly narrating the significance of nature's existence in its natural state and innocence, untainted by human hands, and without blemish, in the form of Huck's escape to freedom. Huck's escape to freedom. (Honjo 68, cited and translated by Taro Maeyashiki)

Honjo describes Huck's behavior as a "natural child's way of life" (59), and says that Huck escaped from the "evils" of society by regarding his own conscience as "good." Yoshiro Higashi's review incorporates a different point of view from the criticisms we have seen so far. In the aforementioned reviews, "nature" refers to the Mississippi, Jackson Island, or, in Kamei's view, the Garden of Eden. However, Higashi does not limit "nature" in Twain's literature to the Mississippi (the "nature" of the outside world), but refers to the "nature" of the spirit, such as Huck's natural conscience. He emphasizes the "wholesomeness in the nature of humanity" (15) and describes how "Huck's determination to help Jim, though he was not aware of it, resulted from the triumph of a sound mind over his conscience" (15). However, he also describes Huck's conscience as follows:

> The story occurs in the pre-Civil War South, where it was a mortal sin to help a runaway slave, let alone keep quiet about it. Huck's conscience is only what he has learned from his environment. Huck's conscience is only what he has acquired from his environment, which means that even the homeless Huck's mind is somewhat warped by the society in which he lives. (Higashi 15-16, cited and translated by Taro Maeyashiki)

In the "Conclusion" section, Higashi describes Huck as "a natural child who dislikes constraints and seeks a free and easy life, but he is not a solitary character" (32). He also explains that he "must be a loving boy who is innocent, gentle, and of sound mind and who is compelled to do good without knowing it" (32). In addition, the fact that he is attracted to "social life" (31) makes it important to recognize that Huck is not a completely natural child, but a "natural man in a social state" who also has civilized elements. There is also a previous study by Keiko Ido, who states that Jim, an African American man who is an important character in this work, is a "natural" (Ido 17).

Other studies in the journal of the Twain Society have discussed the wilderness where the Native Americans lived and the Mississippi River. For example, according to Naoto Sugiyama, Twain was influenced by technological innovations such as railroads, but his free imagination was cultivated during his time as a pilot on the Mississippi River (*Journal of Mark Twain Studies Issue 1*, 52).

In *Huck Finn and Tom Sawyer Among the Indians*, Yasushi Takano sees Twain's depiction of the wilderness inhabited by the Native Americans as a wilderness that makes men lustful, rather than Eden as paradise (*Journal of Mark Twain Studies Issue 10*, 70-77). The reason for this is cited as the Native Americans' involvement in the rape of the white Mills family's daughter Peggy.

The nature of the West is also depicted in the travel books Twain wrote. Hideki Yokoyama interprets the Mississippi River as "a symbol of the flow of time" (228) and "a great natural force far beyond human power" (228), and Huck and Jim are at the mercy of its fate (228). He describes Twain's depiction of nature as follows:

> While nature's capricious mischief is blocked in their path by fog, the river is filled with peaceful pastoral scenes surrounding it and a star-filled sky above the rafts that bob in the river's current. Huck always receives the unspoiled nature of the Mississippi with a realistic sensibility. (228, cited and translated by Taro Maeyashiki)

Yokoyama also portrays Huck as a boy living between nature and civilization (228-229).

In addition, there is an unusual study that attempts to find the relationship between the Twain literature and nature in "fables". As an example, Kazuhiko Tsuji describes the relationship between the Twain literature and nature as follows:

It is not easy to find "nature" in the writings of Mark Twain, an American nationalist writer who was active from the late 19th century to the early 20th century. This is because, contrary to popular belief, Twain was not always a writer who actively sought to engage with nature and to gain something to express from it. Indeed, in several of his travel books, he described nature in the American West, Europe, the Middle East, and the South Pacific, and in his best-known novel, *Adventures of Huckleberry Finn* (1885), he described the majestic Mississippi River based on his own boyhood memories. But he was at his best when he treated nature as a setting for allegory, not when he observed it in detail or in moments of presuppositional reading of nature. (Tsuji 5, cited and translated by Taro Maeyashiki)

According to Tsuji, Twain himself did not have many experiences that could be said to have actually entered the wilderness (5). For example, when Twain described the wilderness in his unfinished work, *Huck and Tom Sawyer Among the Indians* (year of writing: 1884), he referred to multiple sources (7). In other words, it is merely an image constructed from the materials rather than being written based on his actual experiences. In this sense, the depiction of nature extracted from the materials can be said to be "the setting for an allegory" (5).

Some critics do not see nature as a landscape but as a symbol. Lionel Trilling describes the relationship between Huck and the river as follows:

Huck himself is the servant of the river-god, and he comes very close to being aware of the divine nature of the being he serves. (Trilling 108)

We have examined previous studies using "nature" and "civilization" as keywords and the historical background in which Twain lived. Among them, Kamei's "natural children" and Ido's previous studies on "natural man" are closely related to the theme of this book. However, other than these previous studies, there have been almost no serious previous studies on the theme of "natural man," and it is definitely an unexplored field.

So, what is the significance of reading Twain's literature with the keyword "natural man" to begin with? Interestingly, Twain's characters combine elements of both nature and civilization. For example, Tom, the protagonist of *The Adventures of Tom Sawyer* (1876), is a "city boy" (civilized man) in the sense that he is relatively wealthy and grew up in a relatively affluent family. The house in which he lives, the scenery of the town, and the stores that line the streets are all artificial and products of civilization. For Tom, who grew up in a materially well-off environment, living in a natural environment without material goods seems unbearable at first glance. However, even as a civilized man, Tom can enjoy the freedom of Jackson Island's natural surroundings with his other friends. Even after his only means of transportation to his town, a raft, is washed away and he is cut off from civilized society, Tom and his friends on Jackson Island overcome their hardships. He makes the most of his time on Jackson Island. His fascination with observing and interacting with animals and insects, and his ability to live, even for short periods of time, in his own unique dwelling place in the forest, is typical of a naturalist.

Based on these considerations, this paper places Mark Twain's literature in the genealogy of the natural man, analyzes his works from that standpoint, and focuses on the characters to decipher the messages they convey through their works. In the first part, we trace the origins of the natural man, organize the theories of Thomas Hobbes, Jean-Jacques Rousseau, John Locke, and other proponents, and examine their connection to Twain's literature. The second section discusses the elements, ways of life, roles, and messages related to nature as a character. The third section focuses on Twain's depiction of Native Americans, tracing the evolution of Twain's view of Native Americans and exploring the message of his Native American characters. The fourth section examines the relationship between the messages of the characters, including Satan, and religion. By reading Twain's works from the perspective of his natural man characters, we can discover new aspects of his lessons from the past.

PART 1

GENEALOGY OF THE NATURAL MAN

Nature has existed since before human beings. Humans have benefited from nature, but at times, some have suffered natural disasters and lost their lives. Today, countries around the world are suffering from desertification and air pollution caused by deforestation. We must also be prepared for natural disasters such as earthquakes, tsunamis, and heavy rains. However, while heavy rains can cause damage, they can also be a blessing for farmers. Some people believe that the God of all things dwells in nature.

Humans originally took it for granted that they would coexist with nature. However, as Jean-Jacques Rousseau explains in *Discourse on the Origin and Foundations of Inequality* (140-145), when agriculture arose and people began to own private land, a disparity between rich and poor was born. Convenient living has become the norm, and man's connection to nature has become less and less. Over time, people forgot the benefits of nature, promoted the destruction of nature, and became corrupted by greed.

Some scholars sounded the alarm against this human depravity. Civilized man's coexistence with nature required a rethinking of nature itself. It was not until the 16th century that scholars began to propose the image of the natural man as having a conscience nurtured by nature.

CHAPTER 1

PRINCIPAL PROPONENTS AND THEORIES OF THE NATURAL MAN

When we think about the "natural man," we should consider the pre-civilization period and how people lived and coexisted with nature in this era.

In constructing Rousseau's image of natural man along with his hypothesis, we used the book "Reading Emile," written by Nobuhiro Hayashi on the subject of hunting peoples, as a reference. Rousseau is often thought of as the creator of the expression "noble savage." However, according to Ter Ellingson, Rousseau did not actually use the term, nor was he its creator.

> Rousseau is identified not as the original author of Noble Savage but rather as the most effective agent of its promotion. (Ellingson 2)

This image has taken hold because of the savages in Rousseau's *Discourse on the Origin and Foundations of Inequality* (1755), who were interpreted as having a combination of noble elements.

Three of the most famous philosophers who considered the "natural state" as an environment without civilization are the English philosophers Thomas Hobbes (1588-1679) and John Locke (1632-1704) and the French philosopher Jean-Jacques Rousseau (1712-1778), who was born in Geneva and was active in France.

The common attempt of all three was to reconsider or speculate on the legitimacy of past political regimes. By tracing the history from the state of nature, when government did not yet exist, to the current system, these three attempted to uncover the details of the social contract theory between society and man. A graphic representation of their opinions is below.

Three Philosophers' Views on Society and the State

Philosophers	Human view of the state of nature	Vision of the Society and Nation
Thomas Hobbes	Humans are basically equal, but competition (mind), distrust, and pride keep all people at war.	Every person cedes his or her rights to public authority for the sake of self-preservation. The sovereign (sovereign state) uses intimidation and violence to protect against mutual human conflict and foreign enemies.
John Locke	A autonomous being according to natural norms and is not dependent on the permission or will of others. Free, equal, and independent.	Free and equal people submit to political power by agreement with others only to ensure the safety of themselves and their possessions (limited power). People have the right to resist public authority when it fails to fulfill its duties and harms them.
Jean-Jacques Rousseau	The instinct of self-preservation (self-love) and feelings of pity. A happy state of freedom and ignorance of even the idea of right and wrong.	It assumes a public personality (the general will) that always has the common good in mind, not private gain. All people cede their rights to the general will to achieve social order and civil liberties.

(Hatano 211, cited and translated by Taro Maeyashiki)

The chart titled "Three Philosophers' Views on Society and the State" examines the conditions under which human beings would live in a completely free state of nature without government, how they would behave, and what rights they would enjoy. However, each of these three men had their own unique arguments and opinions about the state of nature and rights.

Koichiro Kokubun says that equality in the "state of nature" advocated by Hobbes emphasizes that each person's abilities are not so different from those of others (42). Kokubun states that possession of natural rights by each person determines the beginning of a state of confusion in which people are self-centered and do not consider others (48–49). In other words, according to Gen Nakayama, when people have natural rights, it triggers what Hobbes called "the war of all against all," and a kind of obsession is born, such as the need to kill the other person or to be a winner in order to live (355). This theory is analogous to "original sin," the religious notion that humans are born evil. Hobbes believed that to quell the struggle between human beings, absolute state power is necessary to restrain it. Hobbes explains that when each person's "self-preservation" defense instinct is threatened in the natural state, that defense instinct becomes uncontrollable, causing people to kill each other.

On the other hand, Locke states that the "state of nature" is the rational state of man. He argues that conflict is less likely to occur because humans can make decisions based on reason (Greeson 4-5). He says that because humans are able to act on the basis of reason, they understand equality and the preciousness of the rights to property and life. Locke believed that it was necessary to have such rights protected by the state. However, he advocated that the people should have the right to overthrow the state if it was unjust.

Rousseau, on the other hand, believed that in the state of nature, each person does not threaten the self-preservation of others through having compassion for the affairs of others. In other words, he developed the theory that people live peacefully while living individually, a theory opposite to that of Hobbes. In other words, he advocated the theory that people are born innocent.

From this viewpoint, Rousseau also taught about the "general will." The "general will" is the idea of pursuing the public good as a whole (Kamiya 143), an attitude of trying to implement what everyone agrees with, rather than according to the opinions and claims of individual people. In other words, it is an attempt to seek a goal on which everyone can compromise, rather than think and act in one's own self-interest. This is the basis for Rousseau's pacifism. Rousseau disagrees with the aforementioned opinions of Hobbes and Locke. According to Rousseau, Hobbes and Locke brought the state of society into the state of nature and considered civilization and nature to be one and the same (Nakayama 318-319, 324-325). The state of nature to which Rousseau refers has no civilizational element.

Even though these three models use the same term "state of nature," they differ considerably in their content. Hobbes's state of nature is "a state of struggle between humans" (Greeson 6). Locke's state of nature refers to a state in which human beings are exercising "reason" (Greeson 4). Rousseau's natural state is "a peace among men" (Greeson 4). It is worthwhile to examine these major ideas of the natural state because they provide hints to the embodiment of Twain's imagined nature. If the nature described in Twain's works corresponds to one of the models of the state of nature already mentioned, we may be able to visualize Twain's image of the state of nature and natural man.

CHAPTER 2

TWAIN AND ROUSSEAU'S NATURAL MAN MODEL

Jean-Jacques Rousseau

Illustration by Maurice Quentin de La

(in Public Domain)

So, which of the three models of the natural man, Hobbes, Locke, and Rousseau, presented in Chapter 1 are valid for studying Twain's literature? First, the state of nature as described by Hobbes is for humans to kill each other. However, Twain's characters aim for equality and peace. This agrees with Jean-Jacques Rousseau's state of nature. Locke, like Rousseau, is also based on "born goodness," but he makes an exception. The assumption is that there will be those who take the property rights of others. However, the character Twain portrays is gentle at heart and tries to pursue peace and equality.

Considering the above, Rousseau's natural man is the most appropriate image for examining Twain's literature. If Twain had had the opportunity to come into contact with the works of these three philosophers, we would have a clue as to his character. In fact, Twain had read Rousseau's autobiography (Twain, *Autobiography of Mark Twain Volume 1*, 5). Twain made the following comment on Rousseau's autobiography *The Confessions* (1782).

[…] two autobiographies that Clemens admired.

[…] Rousseau confesses to musturbation, theft, lying, shameful treachery, & attempts made upon his person by Sodomites. (Twain, *Autobiography of Mark Twain. Volume 1*, 6)

In The Confessions, Rousseau wrote about a visit to Saint-Germain, a city in the western suburbs of Paris, France, where he had the opportunity to walk in the woods. In the forest, Rousseau had the following thoughts about natural man:

All day long, I wandered into the forest, seeking and finding remnants of the primitive age there, and tracing its history with great skill. I traced the progress of man's petty falsehoods from the beginning to the end, and by comparing man-made man with natural man, I tried to show people that the true cause of their misfortune lies in the so-called progress and improvement of man-made man. From the heights of my soul, watching my companions blindly following the path of prejudice, negligence, misfortune, and sin, I cried out in a faint voice that they could not hear. Know that all your misfortunes are your own. From this meditation was born the "Theory of the Origin of Human Inequality." (Rousseau, *Confessions*, 378)

Rousseau emphasizes that natural man had to bear the misfortune of "prejudice, negligence, and sin" in the process of becoming a civilized man. It follows that human inequality came about because of the progress of civilization. Rousseau's article *Discourse on the Origin and Foundations of Inequality* (1755) discusses in detail natural man, which is close to primitive man. Rousseau used the French term "l'homme naturel"[2] for natural man, by which he meant "savage." Seven years after publishing

─────────────

[2] (Rousseau, *Discours sur l'Origine et les Fondements de l'Inégalité parmi les Hommes* 21)

this article, in 1762, Rousseau published another educational essay entitled *Emile*, which was also a criticism of civilization. In this work, a teacher encourages Emile to learn the values of nature rather than those of civilization. This is the story of Emile's growth into a natural man. In *Emile*, Rousseau distinguishes between the "natural man living in a natural state" ("l'homme naturel vivant dans l'état de nature," Rousseau, *Emile* 104) and the "natural man living in a social state" ("l'homme naturel vivant dans l'état de société," Rousseau, *Emile*, 104). Rousseau considers Emile to be a "natural man," even though for Rousseau, a natural man would have been a "savage" and not a "white boy" like Emile. More importantly, Rousseau recognized Emile as a natural man with civilized elements. This is noted in *Emile's* statement.

> Il y a bien de la différence entre l'homme naturel vivant dans l'état de nature et l'homme naturel vivant dans l'état de société. Émile n'est pas un sauvage à reléguer dans les deserts; c'est un sauvage fait pour habiter les villes. (Rousseau, *Emile: Ou, De L*'éducation, 104)

> (There is indeed a difference between the natural man living in the state of nature and the natural man living in the state of society. Émile is not a savage to be relegated to the deserts; he's a savage made for cities.) (translated by Taro Maeyashiki)

The above quote shows that Emile is a "natural man" and a "savage" at the same time. In other words, in both *Discourse on the Origin and Foundations of Inequality* and *Emile*, Rousseau's true "natural man" can be interpreted strictly as "natural man, savage". However, because Emile is a natural man living in a social state and educated, his "savage" nature should be less than that of a savage. Therefore, in this paper, we consider Emile, who is not savage but has both civilized and natural elements, to be a natural man-like character.

This is similar to the description "natural man, savage" in Twain's book *The Chronicle of Young Satan* (Twain, *The Mysterious Stranger Manuscript* 139). However, this was not the only time Twain used the term. In fact, around the same time he wrote *The Chronicle of Young Satan,* Twain had an audience with the Austrian emperor, whom he also referred to as a "natural man." In the interview, Twain spoke highly of the emperor and emphasized his natural qualities, which will be described in detail later.

Twain also holds views similar to Rousseau's critique of civilization in *Discourse on the Origin and Foundations of Inequality*, stating:

> In the course of the ages, it [the human race] has built up several great and worshipful civilizations, each bearing deadly gifts which looked like benefits and were welcomed—whereupon the decay and destruction of each of these stately civilizations has followed. (*Culture and Redemption: Religion, the Secular, and American Literature* 155)

According to Twain, man has built a great and respected civilization in changing times. Twain explains, however, that while civilization seemed to have produced benefits, it was a gift that was a gift of death. Hence, he states, corruption and destruction of civilization. In this respect, Twain's opinion agrees with that of Rousseau. Twain points to the corruption of people as follows:

> Whenever man makes a large stride in material prosperity and progress, he is sure to think that he has progressed, whereas he has not advanced an inch; nothing has progressed but his circumstances. He stands where he stood before. He knows more than his forebears, but his character is no improvement upon theirs. (Twain, *Autobiography of Mark Twain. Volume 2*, 371)

Twain states that we are inferior to, not superior to, our ancestors. In view of Twain's view, it makes sense to study his literature using natural man, which is presumed to have existed before civilization, as a keyword. As described above, Rousseau's *The Confessions* is the book that Twain actually read, and Rousseau's natural man model is the closest to the character Twain portrays. Therefore, we will adopt Rousseau's natural man model for this study. However, because Rousseau does not give a clear definition of natural man, we will instead refer to the characteristics of natural man that are generally discussed in the commentaries.

Natural man in *Discourse on the Origin and Foundations of Inequality* and the pre-social boy (natural man) in *Emile* may appear to be of different races and in different environments. However, they are the same in that they are in a natural environment with very few elements of civilization, isolated from society. The following is an explanation of Rousseau's emphasis on natural man, extracted from *Discourse on the Origin and Foundations of Inequality* and *Emile*, with nine keywords in parentheses. However, not all natural man-like characters have all these nine characteristics. Therefore, if more than one of these traits is found in each character, the character is considered as a natural man (target). Natural man-like elements other than the 9 traits are considered 10(x) "other natural man-like elements."

(i) Survival techniques

As is well known, survival skills are the minimum defensive measures necessary to sustain life. Our defensive instincts are inherited from the natural man. Rousseau describes natural man's defensive instincts as follows:

> His [a savage's] self-preservation being almost his only care, his best-trained faculties must be those whose principal object is attack and defense, either to subjugate his prey or to save himself from being the prey of another animal. (*Discourse on the Origin and Foundations of Inequality among Men* 50)

Indeed, at first glance, Rousseau seems to depict natural man living in a peaceful environment in harmony with nature, but he does not say that there are no life-threatening threats around them. They are aware of dangers and try to defend themselves.

Rousseau believes that a good way for adults to help children learn survival skills is to expose them to harsh natural environments.

> One thinks only of preserving one's child. That is not enough. One ought to teach him to preserve himself as a man, to bear the blows of fate, to brave opulence and poverty, to live, if he has to, in freezing Iceland or on Malta's burning rocks. You may very well take precautions against his dying. He will nevertheless have to die. And though his death were not the product of your efforts, still these efforts would be ill conceived. It is less a question of keeping him from dying than of making him live. (*Emile* 42)

The emphasis here is on the fact that having them learn survival skills is a way to maintain vitality.

(ii) Simple desires

The natural man, who has only simple needs, feels happy as long as he can secure food, clothing, and shelter.

> The passions, in turn, derive their origin from our needs and their progress from our knowledge; for one can desire or fear things only through the ideas one can have of them, or by the simple impulse of nature; and savage man, deprived of every kind of enlightenment, experiences only passions of this last kind; his desires do not exceed his physical needs (XI); the only goods he knows in the universe are food, a female, and rest. (*Discourse on the Origin and Foundations of Inequality among Men* 53)

Emile expands upon the desire for simplicity.

> Thus what makes man essentially good is to have few needs an to compare himself little to others: what makes him essentially wicked is to have many needs and to depend very much on opinion. (*Emile* 214)

The quote above describes the difference between asceticism and the multitude of desires. Having simple desires means that you can overcome various desires. In other words, the hurdle to happiness is low.

(iii) The desire for freedom

For Rousseau's depiction of natural man, spiritual and environmental freedom is essential. Rousseau describes freedom for man as follows:

> Without uselessly prolonging these details, everyone must see that, since the bonds of servitude are formed only from the mutual dependence of men and the reciprocal needs that unit them, it is impossible to enslave a man without first putting him in the position of being unable to do without another; a situation which, as it did not exist in the state of nature, leaves each man there free of the yoke, and renders vain the law of the stronger. (*Discourse on the Origin and Foundations of Inequality among Men* 68)

In other words, Rousseau believes that human freedom is limited by dependency or power relations. Emile, on the other hand, states that freedom is strongly associated with "happiness."

It consists in not suffering; health, freedom, and the necessities of life constitute it. (*Discourse on the Origin and Foundations of Inequality among Men* 177)

(iv) Heretical beliefs

Rousseau sees natural man as inheriting innate wisdom from the ancient gods. For example, he states that they know how to use tools without anyone teaching them.

> Let us suppose that without forges and workshops, the tools for farming had fallen from heaven into the hands of the savages, that these men had conquered the mortal hatred they all have for continuous labor, that they had learned to foresee their needs so long in advance, that they had guessed how land must be cultivated, grains sown, and trees planted, that they had discovered the art of grinding wheat and fermenting grapes—all things they would have had to be taught by the gods, as it is impossible to conceive how they could have learned them by themselves. (*Discourse on the Origin and Foundations of Inequality among Men* 54)

According to Rousseau, the natural man is polytheistic and believes that magical wisdom is inherited from the gods (Exit 205). They assume that they know how to use tools without being taught by anyone, instinctively knowing how to use them thanks to the gods. How, then is "heretical belief" interpreted in *Emile*?

> During the first ages men were frightened of everything and saw nothing dead in nature. The idea of matter was formed no less slowly in them than that of spirit , since the former idea is an abstraction itself. They thus filled the universe with gods which could be sensed. Stars, winds, mountains, rivers, trees, cities, even houses, each had its soul, its god, its life. The teraphim of Laban, the manitous of savages, the fetishes of Negroes, all the works of nature and of men,

were the first divinities of mortals. Polytheism was their first religion, and idolatry their first form of worship. (*Emile* 256)

The idea that everything has a soul is the cornerstone of animism. Rousseau's statement, "I found nothing dead in nature," is related to the "rebirth" of natural man in Rousseau's letter to Voltaire, which will be discussed later. Rousseau interprets this as the repeated rebirth of nature without death. Moreover, Rousseau's concept of this rebirth formed because of his "heretical faith." In his "Profession of Faith of the Savoyard Vicar," Rousseau affirmed a natural religion that was heretical from a Christian perspective. The fact is that Rousseau's faith was considered dangerous and *Emile* was banned.

> View the spectacle of nature; hear the inner voice. Has God not told everything to our eyes, to our conscience, to our judgement? (*Emile* 295)

Natural religion seems to be closely involved in Rousseau's construction of the natural man image. Rousseau also says the following about polytheism:

> I am told that a revelation was needed to teach men the way God wanted to be served. They present as proof the diversity of bizarre forms of worship which have been instituted, and do not see that this very diversity comes from the fancifulness of revelations. As soon as peoples took it into their heads to make God speak, each made Him speak in its own way and made Him say what it wanted. If one had listened only to what God says to the heart of man, there would never have been more than one religion on earth. (*Emile* 295)

As the above quote shows, Rousseau did not deny polytheism. Rousseau was originally a Catholic in his beliefs. Christianity's origins are in natural religion, so it would have been familiar to Rousseau (Exit 205). John Scott, a Rousseau scholar, has this to talk about Rousseau's natural religion.

> Rousseau introduces one of his most important authorities almost explicitly as a polytheist, and he implies that the state of innocence is characterized by polytheism. (Scott 6)

It is not surprising that Rousseau was interested in polytheism and that natural man would have the same beliefs. It is also important to note that the "goodness" of man, as Rousseau calls it, derives from polytheism.

We have discussed natural man's religion of nature and confirmed that Rousseau's creed was closely related to it. However, man cannot live by faith alone. Natural man recognized animals as his companions and people.

(v) Animal friendship

Rousseau also mentions the intimate relationship between humans and animals. He explains that they coexisted with the beasts in the forest without being attacked by larger foreign enemies because they were skilled in survival techniques.

> These are no doubt the reasons why negroes and savages worry so little about the wild beasts they might encounter in the woods. In this regard the Caribs of Venezuela, among others, live in the most profound security and without the slightest inconvenience. Although they are most naked, says Francois Correal, they do not hesitate boldly to take their chances in the woods, armed only with bow and arrow; yet no one has ever heard that any of them has been devoured by beasts. (*Discourse on the Origin and Foundations of Inequality* 47-48)

This means that natural man is not at all wary of animals.

We have already mentioned that Rousseau consulted anthropological books when he wrote *Discourse on the Origin and Foundations of Inequality*, and it is certain that he envisioned a utopia in which natural man and animals lived together. So, what does *Emile* say about "animal fellowship"?

> Emile dislikes both turmoil and quarrels, not only among men but even among animals. Never did he incite two dogs to fight with one another, never did he get a dog to chase a cat. This spirit of peace is an effect of his education which, not having fomented *amour-propre* and a high opinion of himself, has diverted him from seeking his pleasures in domination and in another's unhappiness. He suffers when he sees suffering. It is a natural sentiment. (*Emile* 250-251)

Emile not only did not like people fighting, but he did not even like animals fighting and never went out of his way to make them fight as a sideshow. Emile's desire for peace for all is consistent with the pacifism between humans and animals that Rousseau emphasized in *his Discourse on the Origin and Foundations of Inequality.*

(vi) Innocence (conscience rooted in nature)

First, what do "innocence" and "conscience" mean?

Innocence:

1. The state, quality, or virtue of being innocent, especially:

    a. Freedom from sin, moral wrong, or guilt through lack of knowledge of evil.

    b. Guiltlessness of a specific legal crime or offense.

    c. Freedom from guile, cunning, or deceit; simplicity or artlessness.

    d. Lack of worldliness or sophistication; naiveté. (*The American Heritage Dictionary*)

Conscience:

1. a. An awareness of morality in regard to one's behavior; a sense of right and wrong that urges one to act morally: Let your conscience be your guide.

    b. A source of moral or ethical judgment or pronouncement: a document that serves as the nation's conscience.

    c. Conformity to one's own sense of right conduct: a person of unflagging conscience.

2. The part of the superego in psychoanalysis that judges the ethical nature of one's actions and thoughts and then transmits such determinations to the ego for consideration. (*The American Heritage Dictionary*)

Looking at the definitions of "innocence" and "conscience" above, believing in the good without being influenced by circumstances or interests means that one's body and mind are clean and uncontrolled by social influences. In other words, innocence and conscience are closely related.

In Discourse on the Origin and Foundations of Inequality, Rousseau states, "The wild man does not become a bad man because he does not know what it is to be a good man" (Nakayama101). In other words, he instinctively does only good deeds. Rousseau further discusses the importance of the innocent life of the natural man. The French and other Europeans who lived with uncivilized tribes are described as follows:

> [...] whereas one reads in a thousand places that Frenchmen and other Europeans have voluntarily taken refuge among these nations, spent their entire lives there, without any longer being able to leave such a strange way of life and one even sees sensible missionaries regret with emotion the calm and innocent days they spent among such greatly scorned people? If one answers that they do not have enough enlightenment to judge soundly about their state and ours, I will reply that the estimation of happiness is less the affair of reason than of sentiment. Besides, this reply can be turned against us with even more force; for there is a greater distance between our ideas and the mental disposition necessary in order to conceive of the taste that savages find for their way of life than between the ideas of savages and those that can allow them to conceive of our way of life. (*Discourse on the Origin and Foundations of Inequality* 123)

Rousseau says that natural man is not interested in the rest of the world because he is fully satisfied with his life in the savage lands. Hence, when Europeans try to incorporate savages into civilized society, they show little interest. Rousseau, on the contrary, says that Europeans are more attracted to the innocent life of the savages and consequently live with them. Rousseau says that the French and other Europeans chose to live with the savage tribes only because they wanted to continue their "peaceful and innocent life". Feudalism and classism shaped people's status, and the wealthy were corrupted. From such a fallen society, he must have thought that living in a place inhabited by innocent and loving savage tribes would keep his spirit in a healthier state.

So, what was the "innocence" of natural man described in *Emile?* Regarding the nature of man, the teacher Rousseau said to Emile:

> You have enjoyed all the goods nature gave you. Of the ills to which it subjects you and from which I could protect you, you have felt only those which could harden you against other ills. You have known neither hatred nor slavery. Free and contented, you have stayed just and good; for pain and vice are inseparable, and man never becomes wicked except when he is unhappy. (*Emile* 443)

Rousseau's "bondage" here undoubtedly refers to "society," as already mentioned. Rousseau's nature is a peaceful environment without restraints. Therefore, he would have said that if man had lived only in nature, he would not have acquired the wickedness that civilization has brought. In his article "Return to Nature," Rousseau denounces human desires and corrupted spirits, and says that it is important to regain the innocence of the time when we lived in the forest as natural man, to restore the innocence of the primeval origin of mankind and so to purify the human mind, which has been devastated by society, in nature.

If a natural man is innocent and loving, he will naturally be compassionate toward others.

(vii) Compassion

Rousseau's depiction of natural man has "pity" at its core. The following is a quote from Rousseau's description.

> It is pity which instead of that sublime maxim of reasoned justice, *Do unto others as you would have unto you,* inspires all men with this maxim of natural goodness, much less perfect but perhaps more useful than the preceding one: *Do what is good for you with the least possible harm to others.* It is, in a word, in this natural sentiment, rather than in subtle arguments, that one must seek the cause of the repugnance every man would feel in doing evil, even independently of the maxims of education. (*Emile* 64)

To feel pity for others is to possess compassion for them, not harming them unless the situation is life threatening or it is unavoidable, to understand another's position and respect their needs. If such behavior serves to moderate selfish impulses to better serve the species as a whole, it will also act to drive towards a state of mutual respect and equality. A pitying, compassionate natural man must also then be driven towards egalitarianism.

(viii) Egalitarianism

Rousseau's idea of equality was originally established between people in the state of nature.

> It is easy to see that it is in these successive changes to the human constitution that one must seek the first origin of the differences that distinguish men, who, by a common avowal, are naturally as equal among themselves as were the animals of each species, before various physical causes introduced into some species the varieties that we notice among them. (*Discourse on the Origin and Foundations of Inequality* 36-37)

In other words, Rousseau suggests that before differences in physical characteristics were recognized, people were equal. At that time, concepts such as "private property" did not exist, and conditions for inequality were not in place.

When "equal relations" are created, the human world is consequently more peaceful.

(ix) Pacifism

Rousseau's depiction of natural man as having compassion means that he does no harm to others. They are also equal to each other, which creates a state of peace between people and animals.

> But savage man, living dispersed among other animals, and finding himself betimes in a situation to measure his strength with theirs, soon comes to compare himself with them; and, perceiving that he surpasses them more in adroitness than they surpass him in strength, learns to be no longer afraid of them. Set a bear, or a wolf, against a robust, agile, and resolute savage, as they all are, armed with stones and a good cudgel, and you will see that the danger will be at least

on both sides, and that, after a few trials of this kind, wild beasts, which are not fond of attacking each other, will not be at all ready to attack man, whom they will have found to be as wild and ferocious as themselves. With regard to such animals as have really more strength than man has adroitness, he is in the same situation as all weaker animals, which notwithstanding are still able to subsist; except indeed that he has the advantage that, being equally swift of foot, and finding an almost certain place of refuge in every encounter, and thus to fight or fly, as he chooses. Add to this that it does not appear that any animal naturally makes war on man, except in case of self-defence or excessive hunger, or betrays any of those violent antipathies, which seem to indicate that one species is intended by nature for the food of another.(*The Social Contract and Disourse* 101)

This relationship of pacifism is the opposite of the "state of war" advocated by Hobbes. This utopian worldview is Rousseau's idea of the state of nature.

Thus far, we have discussed the characteristics of Rousseau's natural man. However, Rousseau's natural man is only one example of the concept.

"Contemporary illustration to Rousseau's Emile. (18th century)" "The teacher lets his pupil discover and reflect and teaches him to follow nature." by unknown illustrator (in Public Domain)

CHAPTER 3

ROUSSEAU'S NATURAL MAN AND SIMILAR REPRESENTATIONS

Section 1: Green Man and Natural Man

A corbel designed as a foliate head, resembling an acanthus leaf,

that supports the Bamberg Horseman within Bamberg Cathedral,

Germany, from the early 13th century.

By Johannes Otto Först (in Public Domain)

The hypothesis of natural man has been proposed mainly since the 16th century, but there is also the "Green Man" (or "greenman"), which is an ancient representation of the combination of nature and man.

The Green Man was depicted on sculptures in churches and other buildings in medieval Europe. Coulter traces the origin of the Green Man back to Roman times (2nd-century BC).

As a leafy mask in which all or most of the face is composed of leaves, it appears in the late Roman period of the second century AD in which form it makes its first appearance [...]. (Coulter 48)

It is clear from the description here that the Green Man is a representation of a legendary or mythical man whose face is covered with leaves. Rousseau's natural man, however, does not have a face covered with leaves and is more a concrete image of a savage than a representation. There is no legend associated with Rousseau's natural man. Although they seem to have nothing in common, they share the motif of uniting nature and man.

In addition, according to Anderson, there are several forms of Green Man.

In the first and oldest form, he is a male head formed out of a leaf mask; his hair, features, and physiognomy are all made either of a single leaf or of many leaves. In the second form, he is a male head disgorging vegetation from his mouth and often from eyebrows and mustaches. (Anderson 14)

The symbolism of the Green Man includes "rebirth," as Clive Hicks explains (14). Rousseau's natural man is a hypothetical savage who, at first glance, appears to have nothing in common with the Green Man. In fact, however, Rousseau's depiction of natural man is also imbued with the same meaning.

In his 1756 letter to Voltaire on providence, Rousseau explains the natural goodness of life, claiming he has proved it in his description of natural man in the Second Discourse:

I dare to state that there is in the upper Valais not a single Mountaineer discontented with his almost automatic life, and who would not willingly accept, even in place of Paradise, the bargain of being reborn unceasingly in order to vegetate thus in perpetuity. (Rousseau, *Essay on the Origin of Languages and Writings Related to Music*, 575)

Rousseau says that even a lowly peasant would want to be reborn into their previous circumstances and surroundings rather than go to heaven as they, as natural men, know life's "genuine" pleasures.

Section 1: Natural Human Element of Green Man

(i) Survival techniques

The Green Man symbolizes "rebirth" in its origins, as noted above. However, rebirth and natural man's survival, or "trying to survive," have different meanings. Since natural man is not immortal, he hunts and even defends himself against enemies to live day by day, but the Green Man is immortal and has no need to do so.

(ii) Simple desires

The Green Man is commonly associated with images of happiness, such as rebirth or birth, as mentioned earlier. However, it was also a pagan symbol and was a demonic entity in ancient times (Netton 25). Nevertheless, in modern times, it has become a symbol of abundance when celebrating the arrival of spring and a bountiful harvest. However, it is hard to imagine that a symbol for praying for a bountiful harvest tied to profit would be associated with the desire for simplicity.

(iii) The desire for freedom

According to Raymond Foster, a human face is also sometimes etched next to the Green Man face sculpture.

> Around ancient carvings of the Green Man, truly human faces are sometimes to be glimpsed amongst his burgeoning vegetation. These are the green children—the human fruits of spiritual verdure. We are at last in a position to welcome the rebirth of a green child in each one of ourselves. Greenness means free from malign influences. (Foster 189)

(iv) Heretical beliefs

According to Keiji Taga, the religion of the Romans shifted from polytheism to monotheism. During the Roman Empire, there was a mixture of old religions among the Roman and Etruscan citizens of the Empire, as well as among the inhabitants of the empire's colonies and dependencies. (26) Green Man beliefs and their historical background are described as follows:

The concept of the woodland god, the foliate head or Green Man, appears to have followed the Roman armies as they trekked through conquered lands, eventually adopted by the early Christians who aided in the Green Man's spread along trade and pilgrim routes. While early Christian authorities may have used the Green Man image to induce the pagan community to go to church, it is also possible that the early Christian faith did not have a clear definition between the ancient pagan traditions and the new Christian faith, which so heavily borrowed from the past. Because of this lack of definition, the two traditions became fused together—pagan and Christian—co-existing in the same religious structures for hundreds of years. (Varner 154)

(v) Animal friendship

Varner notes the relationship between the Green Man and animals as follows:

> The Green Man is the idea of the Lord of the Wild as he continues to watch over the plants and animals of his kingdom. (Varner 90)

In other words, Varner analyzed the Green Man as being like a king to the plants and animals in the forest. If the Green Man is a king, the other animals are his servants. This is quite different from Rousseau's natural world, where there are no class differences. In Rousseau's utopian world, pacifism is at the core, and all creatures are on equal footing.

(vi) Innocence (conscience rooted in nature)

Does the Green Man possess the innocence of Rousseau's natural man?

> The head of the Green Man was now a reminder of a much more innocent and cohesive time when societies had worked together both for the good of themselves and for the good of Nature. (Curran 181)

Doing what is good for nature and civilization may mean re-discovering the value of nature and finding a balance with civilization, consistent with a conscience rooted in nature.

Section 2: Wild Man

Despite its differences from natural man, the Green Man is consistent with Rousseau's overall conception of natural man, sharing similar symbology and traits such as a desire for rebirth. On the other hand, in medieval Europe, representations based on nature motifs were not limited to the Green Man, but also included the "Wild Man," a "variant of man" (Kambara, "Wild Man Legends: Transformation of Images in the Late Middle Ages (1)," 3). According to Kambara, the Green Man, Snowman, and Santa Claus also belong to the Wild Man category.

According to Kambara, the Wild Man differs from the Green Man in that the Wild Man is not covered with leaves but with hair (Kambara 3, Legend (1)), and half of his body is in the form of a wild beast (Kambara, "Wild Man Legend: Transformation of Images in the Late Middle Ages (2)," 8). The Wild Man's living environment is the mountains of central Europe, such as the Alps (Kambara, "Wild Man Legend: The Transformation of Images in the Late Middle Ages (1)," 4).

The Wild Man shares with the natural man and the Green Man the fact that they live in forests and mountains. They also live in an environment "without rules of life or civilization" (Kambara, "Wild Man Legend: Transformation of Images in the Late Middle Ages (1)," 5), similar to the natural state of the natural man described by Rousseau, where there are no civilized elements. Unlike natural man and the Green Man, however, Wild Man has the element of "cannibalism" (Kambara, "Wild Man Legend: The Transformation of Images in the Late Middle Ages (1)," 9). The natural man has compassion for others, and the Green Man is a symbol of life, spring and autumn harvests, and a guardian deity of human beings. On the other hand, the Wild Man is undoubtedly a natural man of a completely different lineage in that he is a cannibal.

As mentioned briefly in the chapter on "Green Man," natural man is Rousseau's hypothetical image, whereas the Green Man and Wild Man are associated with legends.

A hypothesis is "an assumption in empirical science made to explain a phenomenon in a unified theoretical manner. The truth of the hypothesis is verified by confirming the propositions deduced inevitably from the hypothesis through experiments and observational tests" (Matsumura, 4774, cited and translated by Taro Maeyashiki). Legend, on the other hand, is "a category of oral literature. Legends are those that are told in connection with specific events that people used to believe to be events. It tends to be gradually historicize and rationalized. A legend." (Matsumura 1768, cited and translated by Taro Maeyashiki). Hence, when comparing Rousseau's natural man with the Green Man and the Wild Man, it is necessary to keep in mind the difference between "hypothesis" and "legend." As Koichiro Kokubun mentioned, the natural state described by Rousseau does not exist in history, but only in Rousseau's hypothesis (Kokubun 146). However, Rousseau's depiction of natural man is realistic because he did not construct his image solely on the basis of his own imagination, but rather established it with reference to archeological and anthropological data (Hayashi 200). Thus, hypotheses are analogous to historical artifacts and materials and do not contain narrative elements.

Section 3: Hunters and Natural Man

There are several tribal types of hunter-gatherers. In section 3, we will focus on the Hadza among them and explore their similarities with natural man. The Hadza were chosen from among several tribes because their way of life was outlined in *National Geographic Magazine* (2009). "The Hadza" by Michael Finkel is based on interviews.

Section 1: The Hadza's Characteristics as Natural Man

As already mentioned, Rousseau referred to Buffon's natural history when he imagined natural man (Hayashi Nobuhiro 200). Michael Finkel has researched the Hadza of Tanzania, who are a hunting tribe, and I will analyze their natural man elements according to the outline of his research.

(i) Survival techniques

A tribe member man named Onwas, in his 60s, is described in terms of his survival techniques as follows:

> He [Onwas] has lived all his life in the bush. […] He knows everything there is to know about the bush and virtually nothing of the land beyond. (Finkel 102)

(ii) Simple desires

> They [the Hadza] have no crops, no livestock, no permanent shelter. [...] The Hadza do not engage in warfare. They've never lived densely enough to be seriously threatened by an infectious outbreak. [...] Traditional Hadza, like Onwas and his camp mates, live almost entirely free of possessions. The thing they own—a cooking pot, a water container, an ax—can be wrapped in a blanket and carried over a shoulder. (Finkel 104)

With no crops, livestock, or permanent shelter, and only few personal possessions, the traditional Hadza have little concept of ownership, and do not fight with others for what they have. The boundary for natural man to become civilized is whether he "owns" or not. Therefore, the Hadza's lifestyle is very close to that of natural man, and they have only simple needs.

(iii) The desire for freedom

For the Hadza, freedom, both mentally and physically liberating, is natural and essential.

> They [the Hadza] enjoy an extraordinary amount of leisure time. Anthropologists have estimated that they "work"—actively pursue food—four to six hours a day. (Finkel 104)

The Hadza enjoy their given leisure time to the fullest. According to Finkel, the Hadza also had no social constraints.

> There are things I envy about the Hadza—mostly, how free they appear to be. Free from possessions. Free of most social duties. Free from religious strictures. Free of many family responsibilities. Free from schedules, jobs, bosses, bills, traffic, taxes, news, and money. Free from worry. Free to burp and fart without apology, to grab food and smoke and run shirtless through the thorns. (Finkel 118)

(iv) Heretical beliefs

We know that the Hadza do not have any particular religious holidays or distinct heretical beliefs.

The Hadza are not big on ritual. There is not much room in their lives, it seems, for mysticism, for spirits, for pondering the unknown. There is no specific belief in an afterlife—every Hadza I spoke with said he had no idea what might happen after he died. There are no Hadza priests, shamans or medicine men. (Finkel 113)

When Finkel, the author of this article, asked Onwas about his religious beliefs, he received the following response:

I [Finkel] once asked Onwas to tell me about God, and he said that God was blindingly bright, extremely powerful, and essential for all life. God, he told me, was the sun. (Finkel 113)

However, they are not without ritualistic traditions:

The most important Hadza ritual is the epeme dance, which takes place on moonless nights. Men and women divide into separate groups. The woman sings while the men, one at a time, don a feathered headdress and tie bells around their ankles and strut about, stomping their right foot in time with the singing. Supposedly, on epeme nights, ancestors emerge from the bush and join the dancing. (Finkel 113)

The most important Hadza ritual is the male epeme dance. For more information on epeme, see *The Hadza: Hunter-Gatherers of Tanzania* by Frank Marlowe. What does "epeme" mean? The following is a quote from the book:

Epeme refers to the whole complex of manhood and hunting, but also to the new moon and the relationship between the sexes. (Marlowe 57)

(v) Animal friendship

He [Onwas] can converse with a honeyguide bird, whistling back and forth, and be led directly to a teeming beehive. (Finkel 102)

In the quote above, Finkel has Onwas whistling a conversation with the bird Mitsosie and having Mitsosie take him to the beehive. In addition, James Woodburn says that the Hadza limit the killing of animals for food.

In spite of the large number of species which they are both able to hunt and regarded as edible, the Hadza do not kill very many animals and it is probable that even in the radically reduced area they occupied in 1960 more animals could have been killed of every species without endangering the survival of any species in the area. (Woodburn, *Man the Hunter*, 52)

(vi) Innocence (conscience rooted in nature) and (vii) Compassion

Hunters in general, including the Hadza, can grasp the instinctive behavior of animals in detail when capturing them. They seem to be able to think as if they were an animal, which encourages a conscience and regard for the animal's feelings even when seeking to kill them.

> […] hunter-gatherer societies have evolved an ethic of respect for animals based on the belief that these creatures share many of the morally relevant characteristics of persons. […] In order to become a successful hunter, a person must cultivate a well-developed understanding and knowledge of the animals he intends to kill. He must also use his knowledge of himself to think like the animals and see or sense the world from its point of view. (Henriëtte de Jonge 13)

(viii) Egalitarianism

As we have already discussed, the Hadza have little concept of ownership. In addition:

> No Hadza adult has authority over any other. None has more wealth; or, rather, they all have no wealth. (Finkel 106)

The following is a discussion of the characteristics of natural man that can be said to apply to all hunting people, including the Hadza, which again emphasizes their egalitarian outlook.

> Characteristics of hunter-gatherers include a companionship lifestyle that involves nonexclusive (widely shared) intimacy, characterized by sharing of company, food, residence and movement(Bird-David, 1994; Gibson, 1985; Ingold, 1999). Cooperation, sharing, and egalitarianism are common values. To survive, individuals within the group, whether or not they are kin(and mostly they are not),

cooperate intensely in hunting, gathering, caring for children, and other activities. (*Ancestral Landscapes in Human Evolution* 6-7)

(ix) Pacifism

The scope of the Hadza's activities is now being restricted by outsiders, endangering the tribe and their freedom to follow their traditional way of life. Even then, they are disinclined to fight.

> The Hadza, who by nature are not a combative people, have almost always moved away rather than fight. But now there is nowhere to retreat. There are currently cattle herders in the Hadza bush, and goat herders, and sport hunters, and game poachers. Water holes are fouled by cow excrement. Vegetation is trampled beneath cattle's hooves. Brush is cleared to make way for crops; scarce water is used to irrigate them. Game animals have migrated to national parks, where the Hadza can't follow. Berry groves and trees that attract bees have been destroyed. Over the past century, the Hadza have lost exclusive possession of as much as 90 percent of their homeland. (Finkel 112)

The Hadza, a hunting tribe, has many characteristics of natural man as portrayed by Rousseau. Their ability to act with respect for nature in terms of feeding, simple desires, and the desire for freedom are important factors. These qualities are also critical as they apply to the qualities of Twain's natural man character.

CHAPTER 4

TWAIN'S ASSOCIATION WITH "NATURAL MAN"

I found references to "natural man" in three of the 180 of Twain's works available on the e-book website: (1) a theater review, (2) an interview transcript, and (3) a novel, *The Chronicle of Young Satan*.

(1) "About Play Acting" (theater review)

Around 1898, Twain wrote a theatrical review entitled "About Play Acting". This review is about a play by German playwright Adolf von Wilbrandt called *The Master of Palmyra*. At the beginning of the review, Twain gives his impression of "a remarkable play" (Twain, Hirst ed. 263), followed by a synopsis and discussion of the play's content in which he uses the phrase "natural man". Twain focuses on the Christians and the pagans in the dramatic work, and after giving a synopsis of the content of the work, he adds:

> In the first act the pagans persecute Zoe, the Christian girl, and a pagan mob slaughters her. In the fourth act those same pagans--now very old and zealous--are become Christians, and they persecute the pagans; a mob of them slaughters the pagan youth, Nymphas, who is standing up for the old gods of his fathers. No remark is made about this picturesque failure of civilization; but there it stands, as an unworded suggestion that civilization, even when Christianized, was not able wholly to subdue the natural man in that old day [...]. (Twain, Hirst ed. 268)

In other words, the natural man character Nymphas upholds the gods of his fathers and does not yield to the Christians until the end, emphasizing the pride and nobility of the natural man.

(2) Audience with Emperor Franz Joseph of Austria

During a visit to Austria in 1899, Twain was invited by Franz Joseph (1830-1916), the emperor, to visit his court. After the audience, Twain was interviewed and asked about his impressions of the emperor. Twain describes his impression as follows:

> [...] he struck me as a very fine fellow altogether. Necessarily, he must have a great deal of good, plain, attractive human nature in him. [...] Francis Joseph is just a natural man, although an emperor. [...] I was greatly impressed by him. I liked him very much. I had seen him on several occasions when he was performing public functions. I had not met him before. His face is always the face of a pleasant man, with a kindly good nature. He is a man as well as an emperor - an emperor and a man. (Scharnhorst ed. *Mark Twain: The Complete Interviews* 337)

Twain expresses his liking for the emperor's good nature and says that Franz Joseph is an emperor, a man who is above the clouds, but also very human. Furthermore, in that the emperor has only good and simple desires, he is closer to the natural man proposed by Rousseau.

(3) *The Chronicle of Young Satan*

One of the three manuscripts of *The Mysterious Stranger*, *The Chronicle of Young Satan* (published in 1969, but written between 1897 and 1900), contains the phrase "natural man." In this work, a group of three boys encounter Satan, and their daily lives are transformed. Satan changes the destinies of the boys and the inhabitants of the village. In one scene, Satan addresses the boys, looking back on the history of mankind, scoffing at the foolishness of Christian civilization, and then praising the animals and natural man, who are untainted by it.

We have discussed the philosophers and theories that proposed natural man and the connection between Twain and Rousseau's natural man. We have confirmed that Twain not only read Rousseau's writings but also criticized the same corrupt civilized society. We have also looked at scenes and works in which Twain actually uses the term "natural man". Here, we have confirmed the significance of examining the relationship between Twain's characters and natural man.

In this paper, "natural man character" will be used for "natural man living in a natural state," i.e., Native Americans, and "natural man-like character" for "natural man living in a social state" in which civilized elements can also be found, and Twain's works will be discussed.

In Chapter 1, the major natural state models are listed and discussed. As we have already mentioned, the image of human beings and their thoughts differ depending on the state of nature. Therefore, if we can analyze Twain's conception of the state of nature in his works, it will be easier to understand the significance of his ideas and actions. In the second part of this article, we will discuss specific works, each of which will be discussed with the characteristics of Rousseau's model in mind. We will then examine the message of Twain's natural man character.

PART 2

NATURAL MAN-LIKE CHARACTER QUALITIES AND MESSAGES

In analyzing the natural man character in Part II, the works treated are *The Adventures of Tom Sawyer* 1876, *Adventures of Huckleberry Finn (1885)*, and *Personal Recollections of Joan of Arc (1896)*. In this group of works, we will focus on white characters who have elements of the natural man. Of the characters in this body of work, Huck Finn and Joan of Arc are probably the ones that are particularly close to it. This is because both of them were influenced by the world's values, rules, stereotypes, and other conventions, but they were not enslaved by these conventions, and they were able to follow their own will.

Huck remained a friend of Jim's, unaffected by the pre-Civil War discriminatory attitudes toward African Americans at the time. His act of aiding and abetting slaves proves that Huck had courage. It is also important to note that until he was adopted by the widow Douglas, he was in a relatively free environment despite the agony of his father's violence.

Joan was in an even worse predicament than Huck. Both Huck and Joan lived in different countries and times, but they shared the same commitment to protect the weak. Both of them also believed in their own conscience and maintained their free will.

CHAPTER 1

WHITE CHARACTERS

The nature on which Shunsuke Kamei focuses and the image of Adam in America can be considered a prior study of the theme of my paper. The characters that Twain creates have a rich view of nature, and this view of nature is also Twain's.

The white characters, Tom, Huck, and Joan of Arc, lived through different historical backgrounds, but they were the same in that they lived in a class-based society. Although egalitarianism was the national slogan of the U.S., in reality, it was not egalitarian because prejudice against minorities remained deep-rooted. It is clear that Huck's actions against such minorities are anti-social.

Joan, who was raised in a feudalistic society that was then male-dominated in terms of gender, sacrificed everything to protect the French people, regardless of how she was perceived. Her behavior was also objectively antisocial.

Section 1: The Adventures of Tom Sawyer (1876)

"Tom Sawyer Fishing" (1876)
Illustration by True Williams
(in Public Domain)

The main setting of Twain's early work *The Adventures of Tom Sawyer* is the fictional town of St. Petersburg and Jackson Island. The three boys, Tom, Huck, and Joe, are tired of their normal lives and enjoy a life of freedom and adventure on Jackson Island, far from the town (civilized society). In what ways are these boys natural man-like characters?

Section 1: The Natural Man Element

(i) Survival techniques

The following quote explains how the natural man-like trio protected themselves during the storm scene.

> There was a pause. Now a weird flash turned night into day and showed every little grass-blade, separate and distinct, that grew about their feet. And it showed three white, startled faces, too. A deep peal of thunder went rolling and tumbling down the heavens

and lost itself in sullen rumblings in the distance. A sweep of chilly air passed by, rustling all the leaves and snowing the flaky ashes broadcast about the fire. Another fierce glare lit up the forest and an instant crash followed that seemed to rend the tree-tops right over the boys' heads. They clung together in terror, in the thick gloom that followed. A few big rain-drops fell pattering upon the leaves. (*T.S.*[3] 89-90)

In the above quote, the words "rolling," "tumbling," and "rumbling" are used in a lighthearted rhyme. The storm threatens the boys' safe space, but it is comical, perhaps because of this rhyme. It shows the boys' open-mindednesses that there is no need to be afraid if they face the threat of nature with natural man's survival skills.

This comically expressed storm pass and peace returns. The boys, however, encounter an unexpected event.

But at last the battle was done, and the forces retired with weaker and weaker threatenings and grumblings, and peace resumed her sway. The boys went back to camp, a good deal awed; but they found there was still something to be thankful for, because the great sycamore, the shelter of their beds, was a ruin, now, blasted by the lightnings, and they were not under it when the catastrophe happened. (*T.S.* 90)

How did these three boys, living in a civilized society, survive the elements on Jackson Island? They used a sycamore tree as a shelter. It is natural man-like to consider such a nest. Neither umbrellas nor boots, which are civilized commodities, appear here. The act of sheltering from rain by skillfully using the products of nature on Jackson Island is directly related to natural man's survival techniques.

---

[3]   Abbreviation for *The Adventures of Tom Sawyer.*

An illustration from *The Adventures of Tom Sawyer,* authored by Mark Twain and depicted by True Williams. (in Public Domain)

(ii) Simple desires, (iii) The desire for freedom, (viii) Egalitarianism and (ix) Pacifism

The scene in the quote below is reminiscent of natural man's way of life.

They built a fire against the side of a great log twenty or thirty steps within the sombre depths of the forest, and then cooked some bacon in the frying-pan for supper, and used up half of the corn "pone" stock they had brought. It seemed glorious sport to be feasting in that wild free way in the virgin forest of an unexplored and uninhabited island, far from the haunts of men, and they said they never would return to civilization. (*T.S.* 75)

The flames rising from the bonfire are then described as lighting their faces red, their reddish light shining on the pillared trunks of the forest temple, on the glossy leaves, and on the vines of the floral rope. Jackson Island is Rousseau's ideal natural setting in that it is untouched by civilization.

The three live freely and without interference, catching fish, strolling in the woods, and playing naked in the water. In a normal town, they would have been uncomfortable being naked, but on Jackson Island, it is a natural man's act to try to obtain food by playing in the water and fishing naked without any shame.

The boys also enjoy their freedom on the beaches along the Mississippi River near the forest.

Tom stirred up the other pirates and they all clattered away with a shout, and in a minute or two were stripped and chasing after and tumbling over each other in the shallow limpid water of the white sand-bar. They felt no longing for the little village sleeping in the distance beyond the majestic waste of water. A vagrant current or a slight rise in the river had carried off their raft, but this only gratified them, since its going was something like burning the bridge between them and civilization. (*T.S.* 78)

By nature, the natural man lives naked. The fact that these three boys were raised in a Christian society and stripped naked in this manner is, according to Christian customs, an immodest behavior, but as a natural man, it is the way he really is. This state of mind in which they feel a sense of liberation and joy in life by becoming naked is connected to the praise of American Adam, as mentioned at the beginning of this article.

"A vagrant current or a slight rise in the river had carried off their raft, but this only gratified them, since its going was something like burning the bridge between them and civilization." It would be possible to interpret this as the trio temporarily disconnecting from civilized society and choosing to live in nature. In this regard, the next section will focus on Tom, who relives what a natural man would experience in his natural environment.

This quote is from the scene in which Tom wakes up in the woods on Jackson Island.

When Tom awoke in the morning, he wondered where he was. He sat up and rubbed his eyes and looked around. Then he comprehended. It was the cool gray dawn, and there was a delicious sense of repose and peace in the deep pervading calm and silence of the woods. Not a leaf stirred; not a sound obtruded upon great Nature's meditation. Beaded dew-drops stood upon the leaves and grasses. A white layer of ashes covered the fire, and a thin blue breath of smoke rose straight into the air. Joe and Huck still slept. (*T.S.* 77)

It is not surprising that Tom interprets this as having a monopoly on this mysterious forest without the interference of Huck or Joe. This is similar to the scene in *Adventures of Huckleberry* Finn, where Huck feels like he has the Mississippi River all to himself.

This quote is also typical of natural man's three-person lifestyle:

While Joe was slicing bacon for breakfast, Tom and Huck asked him to hold on a minute; they stepped to a promising nook in the river bank and threw in their lines; almost immediately they had reward. Joe had not had time to get impatient before they were back again with some handsome bass; a couple of sun-perch and a small catfish —provisions enough for quite a family. They fried the fish with the bacon and were astonished; for no fish had ever seemed so delicious before. They did not know that the quicker a fresh water fish is on the fire after he is caught the better he is; and they reflected little upon what a sauce open air sleeping, open air exercise, bathing, and a large ingredient of hunger makes, too. (*T.S.* 78-79)

Activities such as these are difficult to experience in civilized society. Twain's depiction of nature is a special place that gives one a sense of exhilaration and joy that cannot be experienced in away from it.

Tom, Huck, and Joe discover that the townsfolk are conducting a search in the river for their bodies.

Illustration by True Williams (1839-1897)
(in Public Domain)

(iv) Heretical beliefs

Tom and friends did not have the heretical beliefs of natural man, but they were superstitious.

> Next they got their marbles and played "knucks" and "ring-taw" and "keeps" till that amusement grew stale. Then Joe and Huck had another swim, but Tom would not venture, because he found that in kicking off his trousers he had kicked his string of rattlesnake rattles off his ankle, and he wondered how he had escaped cramp so long without the protection of this mysterious charm. He did not venture again until he had found it, and by that time the other boys were tired and ready to rest. (*T.S.* 86)

Tom using the rattlesnake string as a talisman to ward off cramp shows that Tom is superstitious for a white boy who was raised in a Christian community.

The next scene further reveals the natural man's conception of Tom and his friends.

> About midnight Joe awoke, and called the boys. There was a brooding oppressiveness in the air that seemed to bode something. The boys huddled themselves together and sought the friendly companionship of the fire, though the dull dead heat of the breathless atmosphere was stifling. They sat still, intent and waiting. The solemn hush continued. Beyond the light of the fire everything was swallowed up in the blackness of darkness. Presently there came a quivering glow that vaguely revealed the foliage for a moment and then vanished. By and by another came, a little stronger. Then another. Then a faint moan came sighing through the branches of the forest and the boys felt a fleeting breath upon their cheeks, and shuddered with the fancy that the Spirit of the Night had gone by. (*T.S.* 89)

Joe wakes up in the middle of the night, a time when spirits are likely to be present, and all three sense something mysterious in the oppressive air, so they sit motionless by the fire and watch. The expression "the Spirit of the Night had gone by" conveys the boys' tension. The boys felt the presence of a spirit of the forest, the idea of which is not Christian but animistic, according to J. H. Philpot.

> [...] there is a wide range of animistic conceptions connected with tree and forest worship. The tree may be the spirit's perch, or shelter, or favourite haunt; or may serve as a scaffold or altar, where offerings can be set out for some spiritual being; or its shelter may be a place of worship set apart by nature, of some tribes and the only temple, or many tribes, perhaps, the earliest. (Philpot 22)

(v) Animal friendship

Tom and friends co-exist well with the animals, as does natural man, and the following scene depicts the creatures in the forest.

> A tumble-bug came next, heaving sturdily at its ball, and Tom touched the creature, to see it shut its legs against its body and pretend to be dead. The birds were fairly rioting, by this time. A cat-bird, the northern mocker, lit in a tree over Tom's head, and trilled out her imitations of her neighbors in a rapture of enjoyment; then a shrill jay swept down, a flash of blue flame, and stopped on a twig almost within the boy's reach, cocked his head to one side and eyed the strangers with a consuming curiosity; a gray squirrel and a big fellow of the "fox" kind came skurrying along, sitting up at intervals to inspect and chatter at the boys, for the wild things had probably never seen a human being before and scarcely knew whether to be afraid or not. All Nature was wide awake and stirring, now; long lances of sunlight pierced down through the dense foliage far and near, and a few butterflies came fluttering upon the scene. (*T.S.* 78)

In Rousseau's depiction of nature, animals are supposed to be pacifistic and friendly, and this situation is exactly the same. The fox's attempt to communicate with the boys is also interesting. It is possible that the foxes see the boys as their own kind and talk to them.

(viii) Egalitarianism and (ix) Pacifism

The following quote shows three people recovering from homesickness and being active.

They were jubilant with vanity over their new grandeur and the illustrious trouble they were making. They caught fish, cooked supper and ate it [...]. (*T.S.* 81)

The way in which Tom and his friends hunted as much as they wanted and shared their catch together in a friendly manner shows that the boys were equal and were pacifistic and egalitarian. How did life on Jackson Island affect the boys?

After breakfast they went whooping and prancing out on the bar, and chased each other round and round, shedding clothes as they went, until they were naked, and then continued the frolic away up the shoal water of the bar, against the stiff current, which latter tripped their legs from under them from time to time and greatly increased the fun. (*T.S.* 85)

It is fair to say that this scene shows the boys at their most liberated. Here, too, equality and pacifism are emphasized.

(x) Other natural human factors

There are other places where these three boys give the impression of natural man-like elements. An example is their return to camp.

They came back to camp wonderfully refreshed, glad-hearted, and ravenous; and they soon had the camp-fire blazing up again. Huck found a spring of clear cold water close by, and the boys made cups of broad oak or hickory leaves, and felt that water, sweetened with such a wild-wood charm as that, would be a good enough substitute for coffee. (*T.S.* 8)

The boys' idea of making cups from oak trees and hickory leaves is typical of a natural man. Normally, we would drink from pre-made wooden, ceramic, or plastic cups, but these three boys are able to make these natural cups by themselves without being taught. In this sense, these three are natural man-like characters. The following quote also conveys Twain's unique view of nature from the natural world.

They lay around in the shade, after breakfast, while Huck had a smoke, and then went off through the woods on an exploring expedition. They tramped gaily along, over decaying logs, through tangled underbrush, among solemn monarchs of the forest, hung from their crowns to the ground with a drooping regalia of grape-vines. Now and then they came upon snug nooks carpeted with grass and jeweled with flowers. (*T.S.* 79)

This part of the story is like a forest in a fairy tale. The phrase "solemn monarchs" gives a sense of the majesty of the forest, and secluded places covered with grass and flowers scattered like jewels even conjures up the image of a palace in the woods. The king of the forest reminds us of the Green Man, who is connected to the origin of natural man.

This unknown forest, which seems to be still untouched by human hands, is an excellent place for the trio to explore.

They found plenty of things to be delighted with but nothing to be astonished at. They discovered that the island was about three miles long and a quarter of a mile wide, and that the shore it lay closest to was only separated from it by a narrow channel hardly two hundred yards wide. They took a swim about every hour, so it was close upon the middle of the afternoon when they got back to camp. They were too hungry to stop to fish, but they fared sumptuously upon cold ham, and then threw themselves down in the shade to talk. But the talk soon began to drag, and then died. The stillness, the solemnity that brooded in the woods, and the sense of loneliness, began to tell upon the spirits of the boys. (*T.S.* 79)

According to the above, they enjoy freedom from society, which is essential for natural man. Furthermore, Tom's natural man-like observation, which I will explain next, would also be included in the natural man trait.

Now, far away in the woods a bird called; another answered; presently the hammering of a woodpecker was heard. Gradually the cool dim gray of the morning whitened, and as gradually sounds multiplied and life manifested itself. The marvel of Nature shaking off sleep and going to work unfolded itself to the musing boy. A little green worm came crawling over a dewy leaf, lifting two-thirds of his body into the air from time to time and "sniffing around," then proceeding again—for he was measuring, Tom said; and when the worm approached him, of its own accord, he sat as still as a stone, with his hopes rising and falling, by turns, as the creature still came toward him or seemed inclined to go elsewhere; and when at last it considered a painful moment with its curved body in the air and then came decisively down upon Tom's leg and began a journey over him, his whole heart was glad — for that meant that he was going to have a new suit of clothes — without the shadow of a doubt a gaudy piratical uniform. (*T.S.* 77-78)

This kind of observation is not something we are aware of in everyday life. The fact that he knows that the caterpillar's movement is a sign that he can get new clothes is typical of a natural man. He also shares with Huck this belief in superstitions rooted in nature.

In the current scene, a group of ants appear out of nowhere and begin to labor. Here again, we see that Tom has a natural man-like observation.

Now a procession of ants appeared, from nowhere in particular, and went about their labors; one struggled manfully by with a dead spider five times as big as itself in its arms, and lugged it straight up a tree-trunk. A brown spotted lady-bug climbed the dizzy height of a grass blade, and Tom bent down close to it and said, "Lady-bug, lady-bug, fly away home, your house is on fire, your children's alone" and she took wing and went off to see about it — which did not surprise the boy, for he knew of old that this insect was credulous about conflagrations, and he had practiced upon its simplicity more than once. (*T.S.* 78)

These insects are observed in their entirety from Tom's viewpoint. The description of the spider carcass being five times larger than that of the ants is also concrete and easy to imagine. The expression about the ants going "about their labors" also reminds us of the ants in Aesop's fable "The Ant and the Grasshopper". Here we see that the ants are serious workers. Tom's idea of alerting the ladybugs to the fire is humorous, and his detailed observation of the insects is also natural man-like.

As mentioned in the introduction, Tom is a typical "city boy." Yet, when the setting is moved to Jackson Island, Tom lives a natural man-like life with Huck and Joe. He has survival skills, even for a few days, and he lives freely as he pleases.

Section 2: *Adventures of Huckleberry Finn* (1885)[4]

The following is the story of Huck Finn, who, with his fugitive slave Jim, celebrates the great outdoors and the Mississippi River. Published in 1884, this is Twain's middle-period work.

Huck was a vagrant child and grew up abused by his father (Pap). Nonetheless, he was an innocent boy, content with his simple life and living free and easy. However, at the end of his last book, *The Adventures of Tom Sawyer, he* was forcibly adopted by the widow Douglas and was no longer able to live the free life he once enjoyed. Unable to stand the demands of going to school and being bound by the rules of his home, Huck makes up a preposterous incident that leads everyone around him to believe that he was murdered, and he is free to go. This desire for freedom is the reason why critics consider Huck a natural man.

"Huckleberry Finn," portrayed by E. W. Kemble in the first 1884 publication of the novel (in Public)

---

[4] Twain states that *Adventures of Huckleberry Finn* uses various dialects, including the African American Missouri dialect and the Southwestern dialect (Hearn 5). This work uses many dictionary-unscripted words and slang-like terms (Hearn 5).

Section 1: Huckleberry Finn's Prior Studies

Janet Holmgren McKay assesses Huck's relationship with nature as follows:

> In the sunrise passage, for example, Huck's poetic constructions are simple and down-to-earth, reflecting his own experience. He has certainly heard "bull frogs a-cluttering" (onomatopoeia). His frequent night excursions would make him familiar with quiet "like the whole world was asleep" (simile, and his affinity with nature makes his description of "everything smiling in the sun" (personification) totally appropriate. Furthermore, Huck's understanding of nature leads him to present his perception as concrete qualities of the external world. (*H.F.*[5] 70)

McKay notes that Huck narrated poetically, unpretentiously, and honestly about his own experiences in the sunrise scene, and that Huck could certainly hear the frogs because their croaking noise is so realistic.

McKay also says that Huck's nighttime outings may help him become accustomed to the sleeping atmosphere of the world, indicating that Huck is curious about nature and pays attention to its sounds and sights.

Joseph L. Coulombe, author of *Mark Twain and the American West*, describes the natural child Huck's desire for freedom as follows:

> Huck himself is often interpreted as an innocent youth more in touch with the natural world than his nineteenth-century culture. Although taught biases of his age, he ultimately rejected its restrictions by embracing nature and its liberating ethics. His final statement about "lighting out for the Territory[6]" to escape

---

[5] Abbreviation for *Adventures of Huckleberry Finn.*

[6] Although Coulombe does not provide a specific citation in his earlier comment, there are two places in the work where he refers to the Indian Territory: in the letter that Tom wrote impersonating a ruffian, and in the last chapter of the work. Moreover, only in the latter does Huck's intention to go to the Indian Territory appear, so it is possible to identify the quote from Coulombe.

But I reckon I got to light out for the Territory ahead of the rest, because Aunt Sally she's going to adopt me and sivilize me and I can't stand it. I been there before. (296)

Huck's impulse to refuse further indoctrination from Mrs. Douglas and to go to the Indian Territory, a lawless area, can be understood from this quote. As mentioned "sivilization[7]" offered the quintessential formulation of Huck's desire for freedom away from the constraints and abuses of civilization. (113)

From the above quote, we can see that Coulombe focuses on Huck as an innocent young character, more in touch with the natural world, who seeks to escape social constraints by going to Indian territory in search of freedom and liberation.

David Foster has the following to talk about Huck.

While Tom Sawyer is the story of a boy striving to succeed in American society, *The Adventures of Huckleberry Finn* is the story of a boy who wishes to escape from that same society. His dominant impulse is to be free of the restraints and conventions of society and, by implication, thereby to live a more natural life. This impulse receives its severest test as Huck drifts down the Mississippi River on a raft, with an escaping Negro slave. In the equality and relative freedom of life on the raft, a friendship develops, and Huck must confront in himself the moral and psychological consequences of race slavery, perhaps the crucial convention of the civilization he is fleeing. Huck is Twain's natural man. (435)

Foster states that Huck's living with Jim, an African American man, allowed him to build a relationship of equality and friendship that transcended racial boundaries. However, Foster interprets Huck's attempts to help fugitive slaves as going against the slavery of the time and placing

---

above, Indian Territory is a lawless zone. Huck no doubt had a vague idea of this settlement based on the contents of Tom's letter impersonating an outlaw from the Indian Territory. In the sequel, *Huck Finn and Tom Sawyer among the Indians*, he learns more about the settlement and the Native Americans from Tom, and his curiosity is aroused.

[7] The word "sivilization" is used as "sivilize" in *Adventures of Huckleberry Finn*, which critics have nominalized as "sivilization." The critics have noun-ized it. It has been suggested that this is either a misspelling to emphasize Huck's illiteracy or an effect of the dialect. McKay explains this in the same paper as follows.

Twain occasionally has Huck use a dialect spelling, which sometimes reflects a dialect pronunciation, as with sivilize. Huck keeps his distance by misspelling alien forms, and the reader recognizes them as someone else's words and sentiments. (66)

him in a difficult position. Certainly, as Foster indicates, Huck falls into these predicaments. However, Huck chooses to follow his true heart and help Jim in the midst of this adversity. In this passage, Huck's attitude as a natural man who lives freely and obeys no one's orders is expressed. However, there are many other elements of Huck's natural man attitude.

Henry Nash Smith, like Foster, also focuses on Huck's interiority, his conscience rooted in nature.

Henry Nash Smith also endorses "the contrast between the River and the Shore," and then defines Huck: "Basically this character is natural man, pure and spontaneously good" (Coulombe 113)

According to Smith, Huck acts according to his conscience, which is nurtured by nature, even though he is bound by the day-to-day ethical norms of society.

Seiji Honjo also considers Huck a natural child, stating:

Huck escaped from civilized society and played in the woods in search of freedom. He also went to Jackson Island to escape his father, and from there, he went down on a raft with Jim, an African American slave. (Honjo 65, cited and translated by Taro Maeyashiki)

Thus, there are several previous studies that consider Huck a natural child; it is no exaggeration to say that nature raised Huck, since Huck was routinely abused by his father.

Section 2: The Natural Man Element

(i) Survival techniques

Huck has substantial knowledge of nature and excellent skills. He can accurately locate wild strawberries and grapes on Jackson Island.

I went exploring around down through the island. I was boss of it; it all belonged to me, so to say, and I wanted to know all about it; but mainly I wanted to put in the time. I found plenty strawberries, ripe and prime; and green summer-grapes, and green razberries; and the green blackberries was just beginning to show. They would all come handy by and by, I judged. (*H.F.* 51)

Did Huck have innate wisdom? Huck has explored the island with Tom and his friends in *The Adventures of Tom Sawyer*, but this time he is alone in the scene where he finds a significant amount of ripe strawberries, grapes, and raspberries. As a natural man character, Huck's survival skills certainly enhance his survivability. In addition, Huck can determine the direction in which moss grows (71).

[Judith] 'Which side of a tree does the moss grow on?'

[Huck] 'North side.' (71)

What other survival skills did Huck possess? According to the survival guide, the knowledge that moss grows on the north side of the trees would allow him to know which direction he was currently facing. In other words, it serves as a compass (Hawke 378). Even if you are lost, if you know your direction, you will be able to get to where you are trying to go and improve your chances of survival. A story similar to this one appears in Rousseau's *Emile*. As a teacher, Rousseau taught Emile how to live self-sufficiently by having him figure out how to get home when lost in the woods and by having him read *Robinson Crusoe*. Such wisdom is essential for survival, and because Huck has spent more time in nature than the other boys, he is probably more skilled in these survival techniques.

(ii) Simple desires

What desires and wants did Huck have? He wanted a "change." (15) Huck's only wish was to live somewhere else, free and easy.

(iii) The desire for freedom

What were the joys of traveling the Mississippi River for the natural man characters Huck and Jim? A joy was to paddle the raft out to the middle of the river every night and let the current carry them along. Then Huck and Jim would light their pipes and talk about all sorts of things. Both men spent mornings and evenings naked, regardless, and Huck would wear clothes that the parents of Buck, son of the Grangerfords, whom he had made acquaintance with on the trip, had prepared for him. But he was uncomfortable in those clothes. The Mississippi River is a perfect environment for Huck, where he can enjoy a different kind of freedom without the interference of others.

Jim and Huck on their raft," Illustration by E.W. Kemble (in Public Domain)

(iv) Heretical beliefs

Huck believes in and is in awe of nature-related superstitions. The following is a definition of "superstition" as a belief.

1. An irrational belief that an object, action, or circumstance not logically related to a course of events influences its outcome.

2.

    a. A belief, practice, or rite irrationally maintained by ignorance of the laws of nature or by faith in magic or chance.

    b. A fearful or abject state of mind resulting from such ignorance or irrationality.

    c. Idolatry. (*The American Heritage Dictionary*)

Let us see what kind of superstition Huck believes in, specifically, in the following sentence.

> Pretty soon a spider went crawling up my shoulder, and I flipped it off and it lit in the candle; and before I could budge it was all shriveled up. I didn't need anybody to tell me that that was an awful bad sign and would fetch me some bad luck, so I was scared and most shook the clothes off of me. I got up and turned around in my tracks three times and crossed my breast every time; and then I tied up a little lock of my hair with a thread to keep witches away. But I hadn't no confidence. You do that when you've lost a horse-shoe that you've found, instead of nailing it up over the door, but I hadn't ever heard anybody say it was any way to keep off bad luck when you'd killed a spider. (*H.F.* 16)

Huck reflexively flipped off the spider as it climbed over his shoulder. The spider was burned by the candle. Huck's monologue about it being "an awful bad sign" shows that his anxiety and fear are at their peak.

That the spider is a sacred creature is evident from the following quote:

> As the weaver of fate's web, Spider has some potent symbolism for such a tiny creature. Nearly every lunar goddess has a Spider attribute, as do many deities associated with destiny. Among them we find the Egyptian Neith, the Babylonian Ishtar, the Greek Athene, and the Norse Norns. Hinduism and Buddhism both characterize Spider as

an illusionist and creator. In Africa the spider god is wise and great, but it can also be a trickster spirit. (Grimassi 198)

The above quote shows that the spider is a special creature who pieces together destiny, a trait that even the moon goddess has. In Hinduism and Buddhism, the spider is the magician and creator. The spider god is wise and great, which means that he is also the spirit of a magician.

Returning to the spider scene, after this ominous event, Huck made the sign of the cross on his chest and tied his own hair with a string to ward off witches. It is evident that Huck is very knowledgeable about killing spiders as a way to anger of witches.

Witches are understood to have a close connection to the natural world, as Raven Grimassi explains:

For the Witch, maintaining a vital and living connection to the spirits of Nature is of great importance. (Grimassi 6)

Huck is in awe of spiders, creatures of the natural world, and believes in superstition. This suggests that Huck is more inclined to find contact with the natural world than with civilized society, a trait that is characteristic of natural man.

(v) Animal friendship

Huck encounters several squirrels while strolling around Jackson Island, who he describes as "jabbered at me very friendly" (49). The squirrels being "friendly" was Huck's subjective view, and if Huck did not like the animals, this sort of impression would not have been created. Furthermore, the following quote confirms Huck's friendliness to the animals.

[…] and next you've got the full day, and everything smiling in the sun, and the song-birds just going it! (*H.F.* 136)

These scenes make Huck feel cheerful, as is evident from the expression "everything smiling". From these quotations, we can understand that Huck feels a sense of affinity toward animals.

(vi) Innocence (conscience rooted in nature) and (vii) Compassion

Now, let us analyze a passage from *The Adventures of Tom Sawyer* to see what specific experiences Huck went through to develop a conscience against the distorted common sense of society.

> Shortly Tom came upon the juvenile pariah of the village, Huckleberry Finn, son of the town drunkard. Huckleberry was cordially hated and dreaded by all the mothers of the town, because he was idle and lawless and vulgar and bad — and because all their children admired him so, and delighted in his forbidden society, and wished they dared to be like him. (*T.S.* 40)

Huck is a social outcast, the child of a drunken father, disliked by the town's housewives, because he is lazy and unruly. On the other hand, he is respected by the children of the town. Huck's free-spirited nature is similar to the natural man's desire for freedom, but how did it affect the boys around him?

> Tom was like the rest of the respectable boys, in that he envied Huckleberry his gaudy outcast condition, and was under strict orders not to play with him. So he played with him every time he got a chance. Huckleberry was always dressed in the cast-off clothes of full-grown men, and they were in perennial bloom and fluttering with rags. His hat was a vast ruin with a wide crescent lopped out of its brim; his coat, when he wore one, hung nearly to his heels and had the rearward buttons far down the back; but one suspender supported his trousers; the seat of the trousers bagged low and contained nothing, the fringed legs dragged in the dirt when not rolled up.

> Huckleberry came and went, at his own free will. He slept on doorsteps in fine weather and in empty hogsheads in wet; he did not have to go to school or to church, or call any being master or obey anybody; he could go fishing or swimming when and where he chose, and stay as long as it suited him; nobody forbade him to fight; he could sit up as late as he pleased; he was always the first boy that went barefoot in the spring and the last to resume leather in the fall; he never had to wash, nor put on clean clothes; he could swear

wonderfully. In a word, everything that goes to make life precious that boy had. So thought every harassed, hampered, respectable boy in St. Petersburg. (*T.S.* 40)

Tom was envious of Huck's flashy hobo clothes and his relatively free environment; Huck's sense of freedom was unlike any other boy's and could only be fostered in nature. In contrast, the children of the town were forced to live a life of restrictions.

So far, we have seen Huck when he was still living in town, but for the next while, we will examine the process by which Huck met and colluded with Jim, an African American man, on Jackson Island and fled.

As a natural man-like character, Huck did not take the common sense of the time for granted; he is mentally trapped between helping Jim escape and the fact that he is breaking the law. However, he tries to save Jim from the white men chasing the fugitive slaves and from being imprisoned by the Grangerfords and the Phelpses. Such acts are consistent with natural man's thinking.

Not many people would have risked their own lives to save Jim, as Huck did. Turning Jim in would bring rewards and social glory. But Huck's conscience, rooted in nature, held him back from betraying Jim. His actions are truly respectful of the will of the fugitive slave. His antisocial behavior could have led him to be labeled a criminal if he had made a mistake. Huck suffers from this concern, but he chooses to follow his conscience, questioning the slavery in society.

This quote is from a scene in which Huck and Jim are about to head to Illinois when they run into two men.

Right then, along comes a skiff with two men in it with guns, and they stopped and I stopped. One of them says:

[Man]: 'What's that yonder?'

[Huck]:'A piece of a raft,' I says.

[Man]:'Do you belong on it?'

[Huck]: 'Yes, sir.'

[Man]: 'Any men on it?'

[Huck]: 'Only one, sir.'

[Man]: 'Well, there's five niggers run off to-night, up yonder above the head of the bend. Is your man white or black?'

I didn't answer up prompt. I tried to, but the words wouldn't come. I tried for a second or two, to brace up and out with it, but I warn't man enough — hadn't the spunk of a rabbit. I see I was weakening; so I just give up trying, and up and says:

[Huck]: 'He's white.' (*H.F.* 111)

Huck Finn is approached by two men who are looking for runaway African American slaves.

Illustration by Achille Sirouy (in Public Domain)

Huck's action lead to natural man's pity (compassion) as he tries to protect Jim. This scene shows how Huck prioritized his conscience and judgment over the norms of society. He is indeed a Christian God- and Hell-fearing man, and to a certain extent he is trapped by the norms of the world. If those norms were absolute and governed Huck's decisions, he could not have actually taken the action of helping the fugitive slaves. However, to actually do so would have required courage and risk, and there is no doubt that Huck had some knowledge of the Bible, but only a vague understanding of its contents and a rather strong belief in superstition.

This quote shows Huck's indifference to the content of the Bible:

After supper she got out her book and learned me about Moses and the Bulrushers; and I was in a sweat to find out all about him; but by and by she let it out that Moses had been dead a considerable long time; so then I didn't care no more about him; because I don't take no stock in dead people. (*H.F.* 14)

Here, the widow Douglas tells Huck about Moses and while he was initially interested in Moses, he lost interest when he heard that Moses had long since died. In other words, Huck is only interested in living people. Natural man tries to live in the real world rather than by knowledge, and Huck's lack of education and the stereotypes that form in social life make him a natural man.

Now she had got a start, and she went on and told me all about the good place. She said all a body would have to do there was to go around all day long with a harp and sing, forever and ever. So I didn't think much of it. But I never said so. I asked her if she reckoned Tom Sawyer would go there, and she said, not by a considerable sight. I was glad about that, because I wanted him and me to be together. (*H.F.* 16)

In the scene above, Miss Watson brings the subject of heaven to Huck. According to Miss Watson, heaven is a place of harps and singing forever, but Huck has no interest in going there if Tom's going to hell.

As the two quotes above show, Huck's view of Christianity is ambiguous and based on his own beliefs rather than on biblical standards.

(viii) Egalitarianism

He tries to reach the free state of Illinois on a raft with his fugitive slave Jim against the natural backdrop of the Mississippi, but the river's current is so strong that they are swept away to the south. They stop in towns on their journey, but other than those special occasions, they spend their time on the raft right in the middle of the great river. Their way of life is closely connected to nature. For Huck, the African American Jim is both a companion and a friend.

This special friendship is evident when during his travels, Huck impersonates a girl and visits a house. He becomes friends with an aunt there, who happens to have information about Huck and Jim, so he asks around. Then, when he hears that his pursuers are closing in on Jim, he rushes to tell him:

'Git up and hump yourself, Jim! There ain't a minute to lose. They're after us!' (*H.F.* 72)

Huck says that the chase is not closing in on Jim but on "us". In this emergency situation, it is not a joke, but a statement that shows that he really wants to escape with Jim, that he regards Jim as a dear friend.

Section 3: *Personal Recollections of Joan of Arc* (1896)

Joan of Arc. Illustration by Albert Lynch (1903) (in Public Domain)

While the background of Twain's works we have seen so far is the American Wild West, several of his works are set in the European Middle Ages. One of his best-known is his later work, *Personal Recollections of Joan of Arc*. Twain researched Joan of Arc material for 12 years before writing this novel (Rasmussen 278). Therefore, although the novel is a work of fiction, it is based on historical facts, with the exception of the legends. For example:

Joan of Arc chronology[8]

1412: Born in the village of Domrémy, France.

1425: Hears "the voice" for the first time.

1429: Liberation of Orleans. Witnesses the coronation in Reims.

1430: Captured in Compiègne. Sent to Rouen.

1431: Joan's execution by fire

However, while including historical facts Twain portrayed Joan of Arc from the perspective of several fictional characters such as Sieur Louis de Conte and Noël Rainguesson. In this sense, the work can be considered a historical novel (Rasmussen 268-269). According to Hiroshi Okubo, the translator of *Personal Recollections of Joan of Arc,* Jean Francois Alden, who wrote the novel's preface, is also a fictional character (426). Twain also referred to several references[9] in writing the story of Joan of Arc and was most influenced by two books in particular, Janet Tuckey's *Joan of Arc* and Jules Michelet's *Joan of Arc*. Indeed, an examination of Tuckey's *Joan of Arc* reveals that the scene in which Jean "wants holy water" as she is being burned is the same (198). But nowhere in this work of Tackey's is the dragon mentioned by Twain. In Michelet's version, on the other hand, the dragon appears when Michael the Archangel appears (11). However,

---

[8]   Takayama Kazuhiko. *Jeanne d'Arc.* Iwanami Shoten, 2005.

[9]   Marius Sepet, *Jeanne D'Arc* (Tours, 1887); Michelet, *Jeanne D'Arc* (Paris, 1873); Contesse de Chabannes, La ViergeLorraine: *Jeanne D'Arc* (Paris, 1890); Monseigneur Ricard, *Jeanne D'Arc, La Vénérable* (Paris, 1894); Lord Ronald Gower, *Joan of Arc* (London, 1893); John O'Hagan, *Joan of Arc* (London, 1893); and Janet Tuckey, *Joan of Arc, "The Maid"* (London, 1880). (Budd, ed. *On Mark Twain* 74) John Rechard Green's *History of the English People* (LeMaster 570)

Twain's description of the dragon does not match the description of the dragon in the Michelet version, since the dragon is supposed to be a demon that lives in the forest and remains a legend. Joan's statement to the bishop when she dies, "Bishop, I die through you" (215), matches Joan in the Michelet version. However, the phrase "holy water" is not found in the Michelet version. According to Thomas A. Maik, the following quotation indicates that Twain not only drew on historical references when writing Joan's novel but also incorporated original fiction.

Although reliant on his sources for factual details and accuracy of Joan's life, Twain in *Joan of Arc* moves beyond his sources to do what he does best: invent characters, modify details, develop setting and embellish situations, and interpret character. Twain's Joan for example, with her courage, energy, individuality, conviction, and drive is more in keeping with the Protestant American than keeping the medieval Catholic of Michelet's portrayal. In her defiance of rank and status she is different from Tuckey's Joan. (Maik, LeMaster ed. 570)

According to Thomas Maik, Twain's Joan is more Protestant American than Michelet's Catholic *Joan of Arc*, which Twain is said to have read. However, the citation here does not confirm this fact: Joan of Arc wore a ring engraved with Jesus and Mary in Twain's novel. From this, we can infer that Joan of Arc used this ring as a talisman, just as Catholics worship Mary's image in their churches. Hence, Twain's Joan of Arc is more Catholic. In either case, the narrator of Joan's story, Conto is also a historical figure, but Twain has adapted it considerably.

Why Twain chose Joan as his protagonist and turned her into a full-length novel remains a matter of interest to scholars of Twain. In 1896, the year of the novel's publication, Twain had three daughters: 24-year-old Susy, 22-year-old Clara, 22, and Jean, 16. Joan of Arc, the protagonist of the novel, died young at the age of 19. With three daughters, Joan of Arc would have been a natural touchstone for Twain, as she was close to their age and had a short life.

Mark Twain's portrayal of Joan was divine and angelic, and she never lost her grace, no matter how emaciated, until her final execution.

He started this work in Florence, Italy, in 1892 (Kamei 115). Twain completed the novel in Paris between August 1894 and March 1895. However, in August 1896, he lost his beloved eldest daughter Susy to encephalitis (Watanabe 12-13). In fact, the Clemens family stayed in the city of Rouen in 1894 (Rasmussen 285), and according to Linda Morris, around this time Susy went with Twain to visit the place of Joan of Arc's execution. Shortly thereafter, Susy's condition deteriorated.

> When Twain was writing the final book of the novel, which focuses on Joan's imprisonment, trial, and execution, the family traveled to Rouen to visit the site where all this action took place. Susy became ill there, and instead of having a brief visit, the family was forced to stay there a full month while she convalesced. In retrospect, the connection in Twain's mind between his Joan of Arc and his daughter Susy could only have been strengthened by this coincidence. (Morris 120)

Joan was a brave girl who helped the French regain their freedom from England. Twain chose Joan as the subject of his work because, as a young boy, he found a torn copy of Joan's biography on a street in Hannibal (Phipps 313). The book contains a scene in which Joan, while in prison in Rouen, accuses two vicious English soldiers of stealing her clothes, to which the English soldiers respond in a vile manner. Twain seems to think that Joan's endurance was healthy (Phipps 313).

According to Hiroshi Okubo, the narrator of the novel, Sieur Louis de Conte, was a real person who served as Joan's page, and in this work, Twain made Conte the narrator of the story (Okubo 426). This means that the story's setting, in which Conte is Joan's friend, is completely fictional. Twain intentionally chose him as the narrator because the first letter of his last name coincided with the first letter of his real name, Samuel Langhorne Clemens (Okubo 426). This biography of Joan reflects the mixed feelings of love and hate in Twain's life (Okubo 426).

How does Twain's Joan, a courageous woman of integrity, love, good looks, and a lovely personality, play out as a natural man character? Let's start by reading the work. First, let us look at the following quotations.

[...] she was called the Beautiful; and this was not merely because of the extraordinary beauty of her face and form, but because of the loveliness of her character. These names she kept, and one other—the Brave. (*J.A.*[10] 40)

Twain describes Joan as an animistic woman who celebrates nature and believes in fairies in the woods. Put another way, Twain's portrayal of this girl is closer to natural man, as Jason Gary Horn notes in *Mark Twain and William James: Crafting a Free Self*:

> Twain's Joan emerges as an image of perfectly reconciled thought and action, an exemplary marriage of human genius and divine intellect, bold in spirit, pure, good, and true. (Horn 69)

Horn sees Twain's Joan as a pure and clever girl, based on the above quote. She is also said to be smart, calm, composed, and agile. Her ability to solve problems and act resolutely when necessary is also part of her temperament.

> [...] Joan had a cool head, and—the only cool head there—and she took command and brought order out of that chaos. She did her work quickly and with decision and despatch [...]. (*J.A.* 49)

Joan is only 17 years old, but she restores order to chaos with the same calm and poise as her male counterparts. She wins a series of victories against the British.

She is also portrayed as a pious and pure woman who never misses a prayer (Twain 216). She also possesses supernatural abilities, such as the ability to hear angels and make prophecies.

> Several saints come, attended by myriads of angels, and they speak to me; I hear their voices, but others do not. (*J.A.* 65)

The figure of Joan on the battlefield, faithfully conducting God's command, is described as more godly (*J.A.* 355). In addition, she has leadership and leadership skills (*J.A.* 67), knows about geography, and is skilled in tactics (*J.A.* 80).

---

[10]   Abbreviation for *Personal Recollections of Joan of Arc.*

She moved and spoke with energy and decision; there was a strange new fire in her eye, and also a something wholly new and remarkable in her carriage and in the set of her head. This new light in the eye and this new bearing were born of the authority and leadership which had this day been vested in her by the decree of God, and they asserted that authority as plainly as speech could have done it, yet without ostentation or bravado. This calm consciousness of command, and calm unconscious outward expression of it, remained with her thenceforth until her mission was accomplished. (*J.A.* 67)

Twain's portrayal of Joan of Arc thus far reveals an abundance of spirituality and youthfulness with the natural man-like qualities we have discussed.

"Appearance of St. Catherine and Michael to Joan of Arc"

Illustration by Hermann Anton Stilke(1803-1860) (in Public Domain)

There are other survival techniques to consider in Joan's study.

She mapped out the course she would travel toward the King, and did it like a person perfectly versed in geography; and this itinerary of daily marches was so arranged as to avoid here and there peculiarly dangerous regions by flank movements—which showed that she knew her political geography as intimately as she knew her physical geography; yet she had never had a day's schooling, of course, and was without education. (*J.A.* 80)

Joan was always considerate of others and treated even enemy soldiers with kindness (Twain 227).She avoids unnecessary battles as much as possible. She is a woman who never gives up hope, no matter what predicament she finds herself in or what difficulties she encounters. Even during the religious trial, she overwhelmed the theology professors with her brilliant defense.

She answered all questions frankly, and she told all the story of her visions and of her experiences with the angels and what they said to her [...] Seventeen, she was—seventeen, and all alone on her bench by herself, yet was not afraid, but faced that great company of erudite doctors of law and theology, and by the help of no art learned in the schools, but using only the enchantments which were hers by nature, of youth, sincerity, a voice soft and musical, and an eloquence whose source was the heart [...]. (*J.A.*124-125)

Furthermore, Twain describes Joan as an animistic woman who celebrates nature in the forest and believes in fairies. Twain's portrayal of this girl is similar to that of natural man; focusing on Joan's beliefs reveals her heretical side: Joan's belief in fairies and her intimacy with animals may suggest that she is a girl with animistic, supernatural abilities. With the concept of a girl who believes in a nature religion, it becomes clear that she is deeply involved with nature. There was already an earlier study of Joan's heretical beliefs by Albert Stone, which is cited below.

A vision of the Tree appears to Joan in prison and aids her as much as the Holy Voices to meet death. For the Fairy Tree is the sign of Paradise. It is a pagan sign, not specifically Christian, being associated with children, fairies, open fields, and animals of the forest [...].

(Albert Stone. "Joan of Arc." *On Mark Twain*, edited by Louis Budd, 87)

According to Stone, this belief in fairy trees makes Joan more of a heretical believer than a Christian.

If Joan believes in fairies as the ancient Greeks believed in polytheism or as the Japanese believe in eight million gods, her way of life is similar to that of natural man. Few studies have specifically discussed Joan as a natural man-like being, as portrayed by Twain in the critical literature. Therefore, I want to specifically explore Joan's potential as a natural man character. We will examine how Twain's Joan confronts Christian texts and how she comes to be regarded as a heretic.

"Fairy," Illustration by C.E. Brock. (1870–1938)
(in Public Domain)

Section 1: The Natural Man Element

(i) Survival techniques

Joan's survival skills keep her from losing her life, even though she is wounded in repeated battles. When she encounters an enemy officer in Part II, Chapter 4, she skillfully disguises herself as a member of the British army and survives (91-92).

Also, after Joan is captured in Compiègne and the British army is about to take over the town, imagining the massacre that the army will commit, she tries to climb down from the tower where she is being held, and falls. During that time, she is unconscious for three days and survives without eating or drinking anything (Part II, Chapter 1) (307).

"Joan of Arc in Battle" Illustration by Hermann Stilke (in Public Domain)

(ii) Simple desires

When Joan assumes the commander's position, she is encouraged by Queen Yolande to wear beautiful clothes, but Joan pleads to wear simple attire.

> Queen Yolande wanted Joan to make the best possible impression upon the King and the Court, so she was strenuous to have her clothed in the richest stuffs, wrought upon the princeliest pattern and set off with jewels; but in that she had to be disappointed, of course, Joan not being persuaded to it, but begging to be simply and sincerely dressed, as became a servant of God, and one sent upon a mission of a serious sort and grave political import. (*J.A.* 109)

As a commander, it was natural for her to wear extravagant attire, but Joan was not interested. By dressing modestly, she shrugged off greed and showed herself to be a servant of God.

In addition, upon achieving the liberation of Orléans, Charles VII attempts to bestow upon her the honorary name "Du Lis," meaning "of the lily", but she conveys her selfless desire to remain "Joan of Arc" (Part II, Chapter 23).

> [...] The King paused and looked around upon these signs with quite evident satisfaction.) Rise, Joan of Arc, now and henceforth surnamed *Du Lis*, in grateful acknowledgement of the good blow which you have struck for the lilies of France; and they, and the royal crown, and your own victorious sword, fit and fair company for each other, shall be grouped in you *escutcheon* and be and remain the symbol of your high nobility forever.
>
> As my Lady Du Lis rose, the gilded children of privilege passed forward to welcome her to their sacred ranks and call her by new name; but she was troubled, and said these honours were not meet for one of her lowly birth and satisfaction, and by their kind grace she would remain simple Joan of Arc, nothing more—and so be called. (212)

What was fame and honor worth to Joan? When the Dauphin was officially crowned Charles VII after his coronation at Rheims, he tried to get Joan to accept a reward. However, she only expressed the hope that Domrémy village would be exempted from the annual tribute. The king asked her if she had any other wishes, but she did not ask for more (269). These events show that Joan had only simple desires (Part II, Chapter 35).

(iii) The desire for freedom

An element central to Joan's natural man is the desire for freedom. In addition to her other expressions of freedom such as ignoring the gender traditions of the time or physically escaping captivity, Joan even thinks about the freedom of animals before the freedom of people.

> She was hospitable to them all, for an animal was an animal to her, and dear by mere reason of being an animal, no matter about its

sort or social station; and as she would allow no cages, no collars, no fetters, but left the creatures free to come and go as they liked, that contented them and they came. (*J.S.* 33)

Such philanthropic behavior is also associated with the peaceful natural environment that Rousseau refers to as a utopia.

(iv) Heretical beliefs and (vii) Compassion

Heretical belief is not a major element of natural man, but it is an element that should not be overlooked: what did heretical belief mean to Joan? Joan and the villagers believed in the existence of fairies; Joan's use of the "nymphs"; Joan's acts of dancing with the fairies at Bourlemont and hanging garlands on the trees are reminiscent of nature worship (Twain 21).

Joan always had an affection for fairies and cared about them since she was a child.

> As a child she had loved the fairies, she had spoken a pitying word for them when they were banished from their home (*J.S.* 379)

Nature beliefs were not accepted in civilized society. Fairies were considered demons by Christians of the time. Therefore, when a fairy was discovered by a village woman, there was an uproar. Father Fronte, although sympathetic to the fairies, offered a prayer to banish them. With that prayer, the fairies disappeared completely. During this entire process, Joan was in bed with a fever. When she recovered, his prayer was already over. However, as the following quote shows, upon recovery, Joan protested vehemently against Father Fronte.

> 'Then the fairies committed no sin, for there was no intention to commit one, they not knowing that any one was by; and because they were little creatures and could not speak for themselves and say the law was against the intention, not against the innocent act, because they had no friend to think that simple thing for them and say it, they have been sent away from their home forever, and it was wrong, *wrong* to do it!' (*J.A.* 27-28)

We can see the "pity" in her attempts to defend these weak beings. And when they were permanently banished from the forest where they lived, she lamented their misfortune. This heretical belief in the spirits of nature is characteristic of natural man.

(v) Animal friendship, (viii) Egalitarianism and (ix) Pacifism

Natural man's predisposition to cooperate with animals was inherited by Joan; there is a scene in which Joan expresses animal-like anguish while talking to her friends about the signing of the Trois Treaty.

> The distress in Joan's face was like that which one sees in the face of a dumb animal that has received a mortal hurt. The animal bears it, making no complaint; she bore it also, saying no word. (*J.A.* 43)

This quote shows that Joan possesses qualities that could be described as animal expressions; perhaps the fact that Joan possesses animal instincts is a sign that her and the animals are on good terms.

> Little Joan sat on a box apart, and had her bowl and bread on another one, and her pets around her helping. She had more than was usual of them or economical, because all the outcast cats came and took up with her, and homeless or unlovable animals of other kinds heard about it and came, and these spread the matter to the other creatures, and they came also; and as the birds and the other timid wild things of the woods were not afraid of her, but always had an idea she was a friend when they came across her, and generally struck up an acquaintance with her to get invited to the house, she always had samples of those breeds in stock. (*J.A.* 32-33)

(vi). Innocence (conscience rooted in nature)

The following quote describes Joan's personality:

> [...] she was spotlessly pure in mind and body when society in the highest places was foul in both [...]. (*J.A.* 11-12)

Society was in the throes of corruption, but Joan voluntarily kept herself free from its influence and maintained her purity. She did not question God's voice, and she obeyed his orders. Although Joan was brought up in an environment that did not allow her to enjoy learning, she inherited an innate sense of right and wrong and a guiding principle for her life. And because of her innocence from childhood, she was not hostile to the forest fairies, who were considered demonic in the Christian view, but developed a friendly relationship with them.

Joan has much to contribute as a natural man, Although she wanted to live a simple life as a village girl, she fought against the British army to achieve a peaceful life for her people. Joan was not educated, but nature taught her many things. It was these multiple natural man qualities that enabled her to achieve such greatness.

CHAPTER 2

AFRICAN AMERICAN CHARACTER – JIM

"Huckleberry Finn and Jim, on their raft"
Illustration by E.W. Kemble from the 1884 edition (in Public Domain)

Having discussed natural man-like white characters, we will now look at a natural man-like African American character. Jim in *Adventures of Huckleberry Finn* has more experience at the art of living than Huck; Huck can determine the direction from where moss grows, but when he lived temporarily with Jim on Jackson Island, he relied more on Jim. And when storms came, or when Jim was attacked by rattlesnakes or other animals, he followed Jim's directions. Huck, being a white boy, would have received a light punishment even if he had been found, but not in Jim's case; he was a fugitive slave, and considered inferior to whites at the time. The whites, eager to round up the African Americans, were looking for Jim with guns in hand, and a bounty was promised for his capture. Therefore, unless Jim had more survival skills than Huck, there is no doubt that he would not have been able to escape alone.

In analyzing this work from the author's point of view, a previous study served as a reference. It is *Huckleberry Finn's America* (2009) by Shunsuke Kamei. According to this book, at the beginning of the 17th-century, Europeans had two opposing images of the North American continent. One was the image of a frightening continent of wild, primordial wilderness inhabited by savage, uncivilized indigenous peoples. The other was an idyllic paradise of warm, rich lands with innocent, peaceful Indians who welcomed them with open arms (Kamei, "Huckleberry Finn's America," 8-9).

Kamei sees the latter image as the American Adam. This is not the image of Adam exiled from paradise, but the image of a natural man who maintains his innocence in the midst of nature, as Walt Whitman emphasizes. Kamei cites Tarzan as the archetype of the natural man. Tarzan, who is far away from civilization and coexists freely with animals in the forest, is a natural man, and his idyllic lifestyle is close to the image of the American Adam.

The term "American Adam" refers to a mythic concept considered by some critics and scholars to be the central, definitive element of American literature. Its fundamental premise is based on the view of European colonists who saw the New World not only as a heaven from religious persecution but also as a metaphoric garden, a latter day Eden. (Serafin ed. 37)

The American Adam is a mythological concept and a symbol of the natural man in American literature. The original story of the American Adam is related to the history of European colonists. They were persecuted because they were Puritans, and they decided to flee to the American continent, which seemed like heaven, as a place of refuge. For the Pilgrims, forming a new culture in the new land of America was similar to Adam's expulsion from the Garden of Eden for his sin and his new and brighter life in the new land.

For these early colonists, heavily influenced by their belief in the Judeo-Christian Bible as a divinely ordained guide for human behavior, their sojourn to the New World was gradually perceived as a sort of spiritual "second chance." This second garden offered a new beginning, free of the collective error that had pervaded the world since the failure of the first spiritual experiment in that original garden where Adam had succumbed to evil and lost his innocence. (Serafin ed. 37)

The above quote shows that for these colonists, the Bible was an object of absolute trust, and starting life in the Garden of Eden, the Americas, was a second chance. Unlike Adam's loss of innocence and error through sin, the Puritans' attempt was a fresh and hopeful act.

As an allusive figure, one not definitely expressed anywhere in American literature, the American Adam is nonetheless an intrinsic part of American cultural tradition. In his earlier form, he is the optimistic innocent exemplified by Ralph Waldo Emerson, Henry David Thoreau, and Walt Whitman. He is the authentic man, the figure referred to by Emerson as "the plain old Adam, the simple genuine self against the whole world." (Serafin ed. 37)

An innocent Adam, different from the image of the exiled Eden of Paradise, is presented by Ralph Waldo Emerson. Henry David Thoreau and Walt Whitman similarly adopted the concept. According to Emerson, "Old Abnegation Adam" was a man who opposed the whole world. Kamei's identification of Huck and Tom as American Adams may be because they are Adam before he sinned, or Adam who was driven out of paradise and is trying to start life anew.

> Free of the constraints of the past of limitation imposed by centuries of traditions, he is centered on the future and the promise inherent in the very "newness" of America. (Serafin 37)

The encyclopedia further states that the American Adam is an Adam who, unlike the Adam in exile, is not constrained by the traditions of the past, but can dream and fulfill his dreams in the new heaven and new earth, America (the new Eden).

Thus, Mr. Kamei seems to believe that the United States was founded on the two above-mentioned precepts. Given this, it is not surprising that Twain's image of nature is polarized. As Kamei highlights, the U.S. has always grown between civilization and nature. However, there is a crucial difference between natural man and the American Adam discussed in this paper. That is, natural man has a connection with polytheism, or nature belief, rather than monotheism. The American Adam, on the other hand, is an image constructed on the basis of the monotheistic religion of Christianity.

We will now discuss Jim. A more serious critique that defines Jim as a natural man is Arthur Pettit's *Mark Twain and the South*, in which Pettit specifically analyzes Huck's friend Jim, a African American slave, as a supernatural natural man who manipulates the natural world. We will rely on the following quotations to examine Jim as a natural man-like being.

> Huck pretends to be Jim's protector, but Jim is the one who actually lays the groundwork for a satisfactory relationship. His readings of signs of nature are accurate and his folk cures usually work. It is Jim who suggests that they seek higher ground in the cave before the arrival of storm which would have drowned them, Jim who builds the wigwam on the raft captured in the June flood, Jim who finds Pap's body in the floating house of death and shields Huck from the knowledge by covering Pap's face. Throughout the middle part of the novel this natural man of woods and river is the final authority on storms, stars, snakes, and birds. (Pettit 110)

Jim has authority and survival skills in the natural world, and his staying on top of all the signs in nature, building a tent-like shelter, and preparing for storms and floods, are similar to the acts of a natural man. Certainly, we can infer that Jim possesses ancient survival skills, as Pettit says, but Pettit is sanctifying Jim a bit too much.

Other papers that have similar interpretations to Pettit's are listed below. Keiko Ido focuses on Jim's possible magical abilities and considers him not only as a natural man in the natural world but also as a "magician".

The author gives Jim the ability to be a natural man. Although he is black, he is given powers reminiscent of Natty Bumppo, the charming protagonist of Fenimore Cooper's *Leatherstocking Tales*. Huck is also captivated by his magical powers, though they are unprovable by reason or science. On land, he is just a frightened slave hiding from the white man, but on the raft, he becomes a sorcerer, confronting the flow of nature without restraint. He becomes a wizard who can have heart-to-heart conversations with the spirits that govern the entire forest. Jim becomes Huck's trusted guide in nature, taking the place of Huck's real "pap" (father), who is merely a crude civilized man. (Ido 17, cited and translated by Taro Maeyashiki)

The important point here is that Jim takes Huck's place as his parent, and in the sense that he understands Huck's beliefs and echoes them himself; the two are natural men who are destined to share a common destiny.

(i) Survival techniques[11]

Jim identifies the storm front by observing the birds.

Some young birds come along, flying a yard or two at a time and lighting. Jim said it was a sign it was going to rain. He said it was a sign when young chickens flew that way, and so he reckoned it was the same way when young birds done it. (*H.F.* 56)

---

[11]   Taro Maeyashiki. "Mark Twain's Image of African Americans: Jim as a 'natural man' in *Adventures of Huckleberry Finn*." (23)

Huck puts it simply: "Jim never misses any signs. He knows all kinds of signs" (56), a sentence that shows Huck's respect for Jim. This also suggests that Jim is more of a natural man than Huck.

Jim also has other survival skills. He knows that when he is bitten by a rattlesnake, he should first kill the snake, skin its body, roast it over a fire, and then eat it to remove the poison.

> I [Huck] went to the cavern to get some, and found a rattlesnake in there. I killed him [a rattlesnake] and curled him up on the foot of Jim's blanket, ever so natural, thinking there'd be some fun when Jim found him there. Well, by night I forgot all about the snake, and when Jim flung himself down on the blanket while I struck a light, the snake's mate was there, and bit him [Jim].
>
> He jumped up yelling, and the first thing the light showed was the varmint curled up and ready for another spring. I laid him [the rattlesnake] out in a second with a stick, and Jim grabbed pap's whisky-jug and begun to pour it down.
>
> [...]
>
> Jim told me to chop off the snake's head and throw it away, and then skin the body and roast a piece of it. I done it, and he eat it and said it would help cure him. (*H.F.* 63-64)

It is not clear whether whiskey has any antivenom effect, but it is natural man's self-preservation instinct to think of ways to avoid death. And while drinking alcohol to counteract the poison may be a survival technique that the average person could conceive of, skinning the snake, roasting it, and eating it is primitive survival technique that only a natural man could conceive of. Moreover, Jim is a slave in the service of his white master, Miss Watson, and is not in a position to know how to defend himself against such natural threats, yet he has mastered these survival skills.

It is certainly a coping mechanism that only someone who has lived through nature could have come up with, and it underscores Jim's natural nature.

"Jim and Snake" Illustration by E.W. Kemble (in Public domain)

(ii) Simple desires and (iii) The desire for freedom

He [Jim] was saying how the first thing he would do when he got to a free State he would go to saving up money and never spend a single cent, and when he got enough he would buy his wife, which was owned on a farm close to where Miss Watson lived; and then they would both work to buy the two children, and if their master wouldn't sell them, they'd get an Ab'litionist to go and steal them. (*H.F.* 110)

Jim is a man who puts his family's well-being first and would be satisfied as long as his family was free. Jim's emphasis on these basic human needs makes him a natural man.

Furthermore, society sees that Jim should be charged with a felony as a fugitive slave, but is that judgment really correct? Jim knew that his path to freedom could be closed if he made a mistake.

> There warn't nothing to do, now, but to look out sharp for the town, and not pass it without seeing it. He said he'd be mighty sure to see it, because he'd be a free man the minute he seen it, but if he missed it he'd be in a slave country again and no more show for freedom. Every little while he jumps up and says:
>
> "Dah she is!"
>
> But it warn't. It was Jack-o-lanterns, or lightning-bugs; so he set down again, and went to watching, same as before. Jim said it made him all over trembly and feverish to be so close to freedom. (*H.F.* 110)

This scene falls as Huck and Jim are trying to get up the river on the raft, aiming to reach Cairo. Jim knows that if he reaches Cairo, he will be free; however, if he does not, he will revert back to a slave existence. Winning his freedom governs the fate of himself and his family. The thought of freedom makes him feel hot, as if he had a fever, so it was not just a desire to be free, but more like a will.

(iv) Heretical beliefs

What kind of superstitions fascinated Jim? He divines the future with a ball of hair from a cow. Critic Michael Hearn points out that Jim's divination of Huck's future with a hairball has its origins in African and German traditions.

> When an ox licks his hair, it goes down into the left side of the pouch where it forms a ball. It was believed that a hair ball not only could tell the future but might also be used to bewitch others. Ever since ancient times, visceral objects have been thought to possess soothsaying powers; and white hair-ball divination is a voodoo practice(and one of the few examples of Jim's "magic" which is of African origin), it is also a German tradition. (Hearn 49)

The above research provides clues to the origins of Jim's unorthodox ideas. Jim's ancestors are African, as they should be. It is also possible that Jim's ancestors were brought to America from West Africa, since voodoo originated in West Africa. However, the idea that hairballs possess the mysterious power to foretell fortune is related to animism. Hairballs are not man-made; they are a natural product of the animal's body. Jim's connection to nature is not limited to this; his unique ideas about the moon and stars also suggest such a connection.

> We [Huck and Jim] had the sky, up there, all speckled with stars, and we used to lay on our backs and look up at them, and discuss about whether they was made, or only just happened—Jim he allowed they was made, but I allowed they happened; I judged it would have took too long to make so many. Jim said the moon could a laid them; well, that looked kind of reasonable, so I didn't say nothing against it, because I've seen a frog lay most as many, so of course it could be done. We used to watch the stars fell, too, and see them streak down. Jim allowed they'd got spoiled and was hove out of the nest. (*H.F.* 136)

Jim has a natural man's view of the world, as he has a unique interpretation of the birth of the stars, as described above, in a society where creation myths were commonplace, as in the biblical book of Genesis. The idea of a "nest," which reminds us of the natural habitat of birds, is also typical of Jim as a natural man character.

(v) Animal friendship

The following passage shows that Jim is in awe of the animals.

> I was going to catch some of them, but Jim wouldn't let me. He said it was death. He said his father laid mighty sick once, and some of them catched a bird, and his old granny said his father would die, and he did. (*H.F.* 56)

The act of leaving birds alone in their natural habitat without catching them attempts to preserve the harmony of nature. It is also possible that the superstition that one will die if one approaches a bird that makes strange movements, such as flying a little and then stopping, may have arisen out of a sense of reverence for the animal.

(vi) Innocence (conscience rooted in nature)[12] and (vii) Compassion

Jim, like Huck, acted according to his conscience. Huck was a benefactor and a good friend to Jim. Jim put the safety of Huck and Tom above his own personal safety. The following quote is from Tom when he was shot and wounded in the leg, and Tom urged Jim and the others to run away. What Jim said to him at that time is as follows:

> 'Well, den, dis is de way it look to me, Huck. Ef it wuz *him* dat 'uz bein' sot free, en one er de boys wuz to git shot, would he say, 'Go on en save me, nemmine 'bout a doctor f'r to save dis one?' Is dat like Mars Tom Sawyer? Would he say dat? You bet he wouldn't! Well, den, is Jim gywne to say it? No, sah — I doan' budge a step out'n dis place 'dout a doctor, not if it's forty year! (*H.F.*279)

Jim says that if Tom was the one who is trying to get free as he is, it is inconceivable that Tom would abandon his friends to do so. Because of the geographical conditions, Jim was already in the South and would have been caught even if he had escaped in this scene. However, there was still a chance that Jim could escape. Even so, he insists that he will not leave this place, not even for a step, until the doctor arrives. We can recognize that his attitude of not abandoning Tom is a sign of compassion. He is not governed only by his own emotions but by his natural conscience.

(viii) Egalitarianism

The following quote shows that Jim regards Huck as an equal.

> Jim said if we had the canoe hid in a good place, and had all the traps in the cavern, we could rush there if anybody was to come to the island, and they would never find us without dogs. (*H.F.*59)

We have already noted in the second section that Huck also uses the word "us" to include himself and Jim, but here Jim also uses "we" twice and "us "we" is used once. This repetition of the expression "we" emphasize the sense of camaraderie.

---

[12]   T. Maeyashiki. "Mark Twain's Image of African Americans: Jim as 'Natural Man' in *Adventures of Huckleberry Finn.*" (40)

CHAPTER 3

MESSAGES OF NATURAL MAN-LIKE CHARACTERS

Section 1: *The Adventures of Tom Sawyer* (Desire for Freedom)

I have already mentioned that the trio of Huck, Tom, and Joe became natural men, albeit transiently, by temporarily living on Jackson Island, a place far removed from civilized society. They became natural men because, like the Native Americans, they were able to enjoy nature in an unbounded and free environment. Hunting and exploring the forests at their own pace, the three men were truly reliving the life of a natural man. Their message advocates the significance of returning to a natural world filled with freedom and openness rather than a society oppressed by rules and regulations.

Section 2: *Adventures of Huckleberry Finn* (Significance of Freedom)

Huck was adopted by the widow Douglas and forced to live an uncomfortable life with his freedom gone.

> The widow Douglas, she took me for her son, and allowed she would sivilize me; but it was rough living in the house all the time, considering how dismal regular and decent the widow was in all her ways; and so when I couldn't stand it no longer, I lit out. I got into my old rags, and my sugar-hogshead again, and was free and satisfied. But Tom Sawyer he hunted me up and said he was going to start a band of robbers, and I might join if I would go back to the widow and be respectable. So I went back. (*H.F.* 13)

How would Huck feel about having a social life? Huck always wanted to be free to live outside in a liberated place, rather than to lead a life like other people. The desire to be free from bondage is quite simple. Moreover, it does not require money or time to fulfill this desire; it can be fulfilled by simply physically leaving "home".

A passage in *Adventures of Huckleberry Finn makes* Huck's sentiments clear.

> It was kind of lazy and jolly, laying off comfortable all day, smoking and fishing, and no books nor study. Two months or more run along, and my clothes got to be all rags and dirt, and I didn't see how I'd ever got to like it so well at the widow's, where you had to wash, and eat on a plate, and comb up, and go to bed and get up regular, and be forever bothering over a book, and have old Miss Watson pecking at you all the time. I didn't want to go back no more. I had stopped cussing, because the widow didn't like it; but now I took to it again because pap hadn't no objections. It was pretty good times up in the woods there, take it all around. (*H.F.* 36-37)

What change in Huck's state of mind did he experience when he found himself in an environment where he was not bound by society's discipline? In this scene, Huck, living with his violent father, felt more liberated than when he lived with the widow Douglas. The freewheeling lifestyle suited Huck better.

The message of Huck, a natural man-like character, is the importance of focusing on the individual conscience rather than the social conscience and the importance of realizing friendships across racial boundaries. He also argues that an environment constrained by religion and discipline deprives people of spiritual freedom.

The message of the work would be a satire of the U.S. government's approach that contradicts the Christian spirit that drove Jim away, and a reminder that Huck, a boy about 14 years old, not an adult, is capable of a more healthy view of things and that their opinions should not be taken lightly just because they are children.

The story of "Sollermun" Illustration by E.W. Kemble (in Public Domain)

Section 3: *Personal Recollections of Joan of Arc* (Significance of Joan of Arc's Actions)

"Miniature depicting Jeanne d'Arc from The Lives of Famous Women" Illustration by Jean Pichore (in Public Domain)

Joan's attempt to restore the "freedom" of the French can be explained by considering the basic desire of natural man, and the desire for freedom can be seen in the change in Joan's state of mind after she steadily accomplished the mission voiced from heaven, the liberation of Orleans and the crowning of Charles VII in Reims. When Joan completes her mission, she feels as if she is free to return to her heavenly homeland and is immersed in a sense of euphoria. For Rousseau's natural man, freedom is an essential need.

Susan Moller Okin describes Rousseau's "equality" and "freedom" as follows:

> Both in the original state of nature hypothesized in the first part of the *Discourse on Inequality*, and in the education prescribed for *Emile*, independence from others and their opinion is clearly the central value. Like equality, freedom was also a very personal ideal for Rousseau. (Okin 154)

The natural environment is never threatened by natural man. What would happen if their habitat was threatened by the invasion of civilization? At the time, much of France was under British rule, and Joan wanted to achieve French independence from England because she believed that the French would lose all their freedom. Rousseau states in *Discourse on the Origin and Foundations of Inequality* that ownership, one's territory, and land are civilized concepts (Nakayama 123). However, natural man, as Rousseau advocated, celebrated freedom in the vastness of nature, without any restrictions. In the primordial state of nature, the land was for the natural man without limit. He did not have to think about his own or anyone else's territorial rights.

Even for civilized people, freedom can be achieved by securing land on which to live. Without an inherent territory, freedom would not exist, and one would always be forced to be subordinate to other nations and others, as was the case with the Roman vassal states. In Twain's work, Joan emphasizes to the advisors of Charles VII that the territory of France has been drastically reduced and advises that France will lose its homeland if this situation continues. The concept of "territory" is the same as

Rousseau's description of "private property". Private property is a concept linked to the origins of civilization. It causes inequality. However, in terms of freedom from bondage, it is consistent with the freedom sought by natural man.

The growing sense of danger that their land is about to be completely occupied is similar to the sense of danger that hunter-gatherers feel toward their colonizers.[13] As already discussed, Rousseau's image of natural man is similar to that of hunter-gatherers.

Unlike hunters, animals were not food for Joan, but friends. Joan also could put herself in the animals' shoes because of her constant contact with them.

Joan was a natural man before the war, when she was in close contact with the fairies before God's decree. Until the war, she was free to live her life with few constraints from people or divine commands. Joan was a natural man character, living in the midst of nature, at peace with animals, and she saw through the fundamentalist thinking of those who saw in her heretical mixture of Christianity and nature religion a one-sided Satanic authority.

Section 4: *Adventures of Huckleberry Finn* (Jim and Huck's message)

A fugitive slave and a white boy traveling together would have been remarkable for Americans in the slave society of the South at the time. Jim's act of running away was accomplished because he was able to question and change his thinking about the way the world was. This is evident in the fact that the white boy and the African American man had formed a friendship. However, Twain's new framework of the natural man character conveys his attempt to value these two people of different races

---

[13] In Chapter 3 (Section 3) of Part I, the Hadza of Tanzania were warm-hearted hunters who did not kill except for prey to survive. However, in recent years, their previous peace has been threatened by the rapid loss of their land and the influence of foreign cultures due to invasions from the outside. To maintain the peace that had been maintained until then, it became necessary to assimilate into other cultures or to show some form of resistance. However, a peaceful solution has yet to be found (*National Geographic*, December 12, 2009).

as equals. It is well known that Twain, who was critical of imperialism and colonialism, was friendly with African Americans from an early age. Twain's decision to introduce these two characters was a radical reversal of the ethics of the time, when judging a person's worth solely on the basis of his or her race was considered acceptable discrimination. By setting them as equal natural man-like characters, Twain may have conveyed the importance of transcending racial boundaries.

Section 5: Twain's View of Nature

Did Twain, the creator of the natural man-like characters Tom and Huck also have natural man elements? In fact, Twain was a writer who experienced both the harshness and the benefits of nature. As a boy, he developed a sensitivity to the beauty of nature in the countryside.

Chapter 4 of Twain's autobiography contains a poetic and detailed description of the natural beauty of the countryside.

> I can call back the solemn twilight and mystery of the deep woods, the earthy smells, the faint odors of the wild flowers, the sheen of rainwashed foliage, the rattling clatter of drops when the wind shook the trees, the far-off hammering of woodpeckers and the muffled drumming of wood pheasants in the remoteness of the forest, the snapshot glimpses of disturbed wild creatures scurrying through the grass [...]. (Twain, *The Autobiography of Mark Twain* 16)

As an adult, he became a pilot on the Mississippi River and kept passengers safe in the wilderness. In this sense, he is a natural man. Twain spent his boyhood in the Midwestern town of Hannibal, and it is no exaggeration to say that it was here that Twain formed his character.

Twain satirizes in his works the political world and people's thinking corrupted by post-Civil War monetary universalism, and emphasizes the importance of returning to the natural, socially unbounded way of thinking about things through characters such as Huck, Jim, Joan of Arc, and the Native Americans. Twain himself has both natural and civilized values and perspectives because of his influences from Hannibal in the wilderness to civilized Eastern society. In other words, Twain also searched for a balance between nature and civilization. Kamei succinctly summarizes Twain's western values cultivated in Hannibal and later eastern values as follows:

Western Values: Nature, Freedom, and Wild

Eastern Values: Civilization, Order, and Culture

(Kamei, *The World of Mark Twain*, 148)

Twain's own natural man-like qualities are undeniable, given that he grew up in rural surroundings as a boy. Rousseau's depiction of natural man changes from a selfless, freedom-seeking existence in nature to one that emphasizes civilized values such as "private property" (Qvortrup 35). Twain's shift of his base of operations from the West to the East certainly made him more of a civilized man than a natural man. What is important to note here, however, is that Twain retained some natural man elements throughout his life. Evidence for this is clear from the many natural elements in his later works. Furthermore, Twain's desire for freedom is also a natural man element.

> A pilot, in those days, was the only unfettered and entirely independent human being in the earth. (Dempsey 225)

> For Twain, his time as a pilot shows a life of liberation and freedom.

Section 6: Twain's Survival Techniques

The same can be said for survival skills. Pilots must be familiar with regulations and rules, check water depths, know distances and obstructions, know how to maneuver, signal, and navigate the vessel with knowledge of the technology and signs, and always keep the safety of passengers in mind.

> Mark Twain tells of three indispensable survival skills for a river pilot: Pay attention, read beyond the surface, and be ready for change. (*The New Georgia Guide* 134)

> Pilotage is not an easy job. As mentioned in the introduction, the pseudonym "Mark Twain" refers to a depth of 2 fathoms, or 3.6 meters below the surface, the level at which a steamboat can safely sail. This suggests that Twain was always interested in survival.

As we have discussed, we can see that Twain himself was a natural man-like being, not only in his survival skills and desire for freedom, but also in his observation of nature. As noted in the introduction, Twain had some civilized traits, such as building a mansion and trying to dig for silver in 1874, but before the Civil War, pilotage was an occupation that natural man would have preferred. The experience he gained on the Mississippi River would influence Twain for years to come.

PART 3

TWAIN AND THE MESSAGE OF NATIVE AMERICANS (NATURAL MAN)

The purpose of this third section is to clarify Twain's message by analyzing how he represents the Native American as natural man in his works. Among them, Koji Tabei's article "From White to Red: Mark Twain and the American Indian" discusses Twain's changing views on Indians and elaborates on how the transformation of his views on Native Americans was reflected in his writings. This article discusses Twain's changing views of Native Americans and how these changing views were reflected in his writings. In this article, Twain's view of Native Americans wavered from youth to middle age, but in his later work, "Extracts from Captain Stormfield's Visit to Heaven," Twain "became a sorcerer of heaven, destroyed sin, banished the demons of prejudice, abandoned white America, and made red America his rightful home," as mentioned by Tabei (336). In discussing the evolution of Twain's view of Native Americans, the author cites the writings of critics such as Richard I. Dodge and Francis Parkman, who Twain is said to have been influenced by. This article provides an overview of the "From White to Red" article and then examines Twain's works on Native Americans, including the author's own viewpoint.

CHAPTER 1

TWAIN'S NATIVE AMERICAN IMAGE

The Native American is closest to the natural man described by Rousseau in Part I. The Native Americans in Twain's works, however, is Injun Joe of *The Adventures of Tom* Sawyer. From the author's point of view, the Native American imagined in Injun Joe is quite different from Rousseau's idealistic, pacifistic, and egalitarian image of natural man.

Section 1: Injun Joe's Inferiority

First, as mentioned earlier, I would like to focus on Injun Joe in *The Adventures of Tom Sawyer*, a relatively early work by Twain. Tabei says that Injun Joe, an Native American, is described as "a thug who has killed many people" (282) and as "of mixed Indian and white descent" (283). This quote is from a scene in which Tom and Huck are talking about Injun Joe.

[Tom] […] Say, Huck, I know another o' them voices; it's Injun Joe.'

[Huck]: 'That's so—that murderin' half-breed! I'd druther they was devils a dern sight. What kin they be up to?' (*T.S.* 56)

Huck states that Injun Joe is the devil incarnate and even commits murder. Twain wrote this work in 1876 after meeting the Goshute tribe. As Tabei notes, this encounter with the tribe distorted Twain's view of the Native Americans (Tabei 269). In a previous study of Injun Joe, Katsumi Satouchi noted, "The Indians were simply a 'savage' to Twain at this time":

One thing to remember about this "Indian," perhaps the most famous in American literary history, is that he is not portrayed as less "Indian" because of his mixed blood than a pure-blood native. In contrast, Injun Joe is portrayed as a more abhorrent "Indian" because of his mixed blood. This negative view of miscegenation was a powerful force in the American popular imagination of the time. Injun Joe is portrayed as a more abhorrent "Indian" because he is of a mixed race. (Satouchi 470-471, cited and translated by Taro Maeyashiki)

It is hard to deny that Twain's image of Native Americans was also born from this kind of herd mentality.

Injun Joe is a murderer, but his reasons for committing the murders cannot be categorized as evil. The following is a quote from Injun Joe's reasons for killing doctor Robinson.

'Five years ago you drove me [Injun Joe] away from your father's kitchen one night, when I come to ask for something to eat, and you [Dr. Robinson] said I warn't there for any good; and when I swore I'd get even with you if it took a hundred years, your father had me jailed for a vagrant. Did you think I'd forget? The Injun blood ain't in me for nothing. […]. (*T.S.* 57)

Rousseau said that natural man is innocent and good; Injun Joe must have been so when he was born. However, society and civilization have caused Injun Joe to lose his natural manliness and become corrupted by social ills. Furthermore, he could not even find food, which is essential for natural man. Can we blame only his own shortsightedness for the cause of his murderous act, as he foresaw the danger of starvation and death? It is undeniable that social ills existed in the background, and the prejudices created by these ills may have distorted Injun Joe's personality.

Section 2: Twain's Changing Views of Native Americans

Section 1: Cooper's depiction of noble Native Americans

In *Huck Finn and Tom Sawyer Among the Indians,* Tabei notes that Tom's image of the noble Native American was tarnished after the tragedy in which the Native Americans killed most of the white Mills family (312-313). What was the image of Native Americans for Tom originally? In the wake of the murder of the white family, Huck questions the idealized image of Native Americans that he had heard from Tom because the reality is so different from it. Huck asks Tom what led him to have a favorable image of Native Americans. Tom replies that it was from the novels of James Fennimore Cooper (1789-1851) (312-313).

"Ball players" "a hand-colored lithograph" Illustration by George Catlin (in Public Domain)

'You reckon maybe you've been mistaken. Well, you have. Injuns ornery! It's the most ignorant idea that ever—why, Jim, they're the noblest human beings that's ever been in the world. If a white man tells you a thing, do you know it's true? No, you don't; because generally it's a lie. But if an Injun tells you a thing, you can bet on it every time for the petrified fact; because you can't get an Injun to lie, he would cut his tongue out first. If you trust to a white man's honor, you better look out; but you trust to an Injun's honor, and nothing in the world can make him betray you would die first, and be glad to. An Injun is all honor. It's what they're made of. You ask a white man to divide his property with you–will he do it? I think I see him at it; but you go to an Injun, and he'll give you everything he's got in the world.

It's just the difference between an Injun and a white man. They're just all generousness and unstingeableness. (35)

In the quote above, Tom tries hard to explain Jim, who hates Native Americans, how to remove his preconceived notions. According to Tom, Native Americans are the "noblest people" in the world and do not lie. He says Native Americans are more trustworthy than whites. He also appreciates their generosity. These Native Americans were certainly Twain's ideal image of Native Americans before he met the Goshutes.

Section 2: Depiction of the degrading appearance of Native Americans

According to Tabei, in *Roughing it* (1870-1871), Twain's encounter with the Goshutes and seeing their reality destroyed his idealized image of Native Americans, and he became extremely disgusted and disillusioned with them (269-270). Twain harshly criticized the Native Americans in his book *The Noble Red Man* (1870). Tabei analyzes Twain's intentions in writing this work.

> It openly revolts against the romanticized view of Indians up to now, and rubbishes "humanitarians" who have been seduced by the image of the "noble red race." (Tabei 6, cited and translated by Taro Maeyashiki)

Tabei says that Twain emphasized the "true character," "violence," and "brutality" of the Native Americans (274-275). According to him, this view of Native Americans did not change from the 1860s to the 1970s (276). A work that influenced Twain's view of Native Americans is Richard Irving Dodge's *Our Wild Indians: Thirty-Three Years' Personal Experience among the Red Men of the Great West - A Popular Account of Their Social Life, Religion, Habits, Traits, Customs, Exploits, etc.*, and Francis Parkman's *Oregon Tail* (277-278). Parkman shares "a viewpoint that sees whites as victims of cruel and inhumane Indians" (280). The fact is that these books accelerated Twain's dislike of Native Americans (277). How, then, does Twain's specific body of work reflect his view of Native Americans?

In *The Adventures of Tom Sawyer* (1876), Tabei says that the Indian game shows Native Americans cruelty and Twain's prejudice (282).

In addition to *The Adventures of Tom Sawyer*, Twain wrote an unfinished book about Native Americans, *Huck Finn & Tom Sawyer Among the Indians*. A synopsis of this follows.

Tom and Huck met the Mills family, five white settlers on their way to Oregon, who would travel with Huck and Tom along the way. When they encounter a group of Native Americans, they are initially welcomed and have a good time. Unbeknownst to Huck and the others, however, the Native Americans' behavior changes, and they suddenly go berserk and slaughter all of the Mills family except Peggy and her sister. An earlier study of this work, "Mark Twain's Unfinished Works: *Huck Finn and Tom Sawyer Among the Indians*: A Journey into Memory and Deep Psychology," by Yuko Yamamoto, like Tabei, touches on the cruelty of the Native Americans. Yamamoto states that the white man's satanic Native Americans image is projected onto this work as follows:

> Anecdotes and gossip about brutal Indians burning with vengeance and torturing maidens like Peggy out of hatred for whites were repeated in various books, reinforcing the image of Indians as demons and enemies of whites. It is said that this reflected the white man's ideology of appealing to the cause of defeating the Indians. (Yamamoto 177, cited and translated by Taro Maeyashiki)

As the quote above shows, the demonization of the Native Americans image was accelerated by the sexual violence of Native Americans against white girls. As Tabei notes, there is no doubt that Twain was a humorist who devoted his energies to "depicting the lowliness of Indians in an amusing way, with 'hooey' and jokes" (Tabei 289).

Section 3: Twain's Fellowship with Native Americans

As we have seen, it is true that demonizing Native Americans was mainstream at the time. But was Twain's portrayal of Native Americans always negative? Twain's portrayal of Native American nature is profound:

in the following scene from *The Adventures of Tom Sawyer,* Huck, Tom, and Joe each play the role of tribal chief, imitate war, and reconcile.

> They assembled in camp toward supper time, hungry and happy; but now a difficulty arose — hostile Indians could not break the bread of hospitality together without first making peace, and this was a simple impossibility without smoking a pipe of peace. There was no other process that ever they had heard of. Two of the savages almost wished they had remained pirates. However, there was no other way; so with such show of cheerfulness as they could muster they called for the pipe and took their whiff as it passed, in due form. (*T.S.* 91)

These three fictional tribal leaders (Huck, Tom, and Joe), who fought as enemies, forgive each other and have dinner together with good humor. This scene shows the friendly and equal relationship between the natural men. Twain's image of natural man is not entirely cruel but also idyllic. It is also important to note that as natural man characters, the three share a space of physical and emotional freedom, unbounded by anyone else. Tom and friends have found in nature a meaning of freedom that has been forgotten in our society. Having seen the scene in which Huck and the trio dress up as Native Americans, let us now consider Injun Joe, who appears in the same book, from the perspective of Rousseau's natural man.

As I have already mentioned, Injun Joe in the first half of *The Adventures of Tom Sawyer* is portrayed as a cruel devil. How about the second half of the book? Here we see a slightly different side of Injun Joe. The next scene describes Joe's attempts to survive after being trapped in a cave.

> He [Injun Joe] had also contrived to catch a few bats, and these, also, he had eaten, leaving only their claws. The poor unfortunate had starved to death. In one place, near at hand, a stalagmite had been slowly growing up from the ground for ages, builded by the water-drip from a stalactite overhead. The captive had broken off the stalagmite, and upon the stump had placed a stone, wherein he had scooped a shallow hollow to catch the precious drop that fell once in every three minutes with the dreary regularity of a clock-tick — a dessert spoonful once in four and twenty hours. (*T.S.* 156)

Those who witnessed this scene wept at the end of Injun Joe's life and signed a petition to have him pardoned for his crimes. According to Tabei, Twain harshly condemns them as "sentimental" and "soft" (284). This passage confirms what Tabei says about Twain's prejudice. Twain's narration does not fall into sentimentalism, as Tabei suggests (Tabei 284). This is because after this quote, when referring to Joe, he calls him "this flitting human insect" (157).

There were other previous studies on Injun Joe in this scene, which are cited below.

> Joe was also trapped in a cave, and he resorted to eating bats and candles before finally dying of starvation. In the novel, Twain presented the horrible death as entirely justified. No longer starting with the premise—as in the 1863 sketch—that America Indians can be grievously wronged, he transformed the tragedy into a sensational and titillating example of poetic justice done to a stereotypically sadistic nonwhite. (Coulombe 97-98)

Coulombe's view is similar to Tabei's, that Twain writes Injun Joe as deserving to die. However, while Twain's view of the Native Americans at this time can be said to be full of contempt, his description of Joe here is sympathetic, as he writes, "The poor unfortunate had starved to death" (156). The following passage may also be an indication of the good impression Twain had of the Native Americans when he read Cooper's novel.

> It is many and many a year since the hapless half-breed scooped out the stone to catch the priceless drops, but to this day the tourist stares longest at that pathetic stone and that dropping water when he comes to see the wonders of McDougal's cave. Injun Joe's Cup stands first in the list of the cavern's marvels; even "Aladdin's Palace" cannot rival it. (157)

Injun Joe's description is almost pejorative, but here we see some respect for Twain's Native Americans.

Tabei says that although Twain was a harsh critic of the Native Americans, he was certainly aware of their plight (291-292). However,

Twain, thinking from the white man's point of view, considered the assault of Native Americans on whites to be inexcusable, and he had no room for sympathy (292). Twain's views on Native Americans, however, gradually shifted, and according to Tabei's analysis, Twain "began to have an Indian perspective as early as 1881." Tabei focuses on the content of a speech Twain gave in 1881. The following is Tabei's description (with accompanying translation) and the content of the lecture.

Twain was invited to speak at the New England Society dinner in Philadelphia. The dinner was a celebration of the landing of the Pilgrim Fathers in Plymouth in 1620. At the banquet, Twain gave a speech that the distinguished guests there were appalled by. "What do you want to celebrate them for? Your pardon: the gentleman at my left assures me that you are not celebrating the Pilgrims themselves, but the landing of the Pilgrims at Plymouth Rock on the 22d of December. Why, the other pretext was thin enough, but

this is thinner than ever; the other was tissue, tinfoil, fish-bladder, but this is gold-leaf. Celebrating their landing! What was there remarkable about it, I would like to know?" (94) He begins challengingly. "My ancestors were not Pilgrims," Twain says.

"My first American ancestor, gentlemen, was an Indian- an early Indian. Your ancestors skinned him alive, and I am an orphan. Not one drop of my blood flows in that Indian's veins today. My first American ancestors, gentlemen, were Indians, and early Indians at that. Your ancestors scalped that Indian alive. Therefore I am an orphan. Today, there is no drop of my blood in the veins of an Indian. I stand here, lone and forlorn, without an ancestor." […] And he said, "I ask you to put yourselves in his place. I ask it as a favor; I ask it as a tardy act of justice" ("From White to Red," 303-304, cited and translated by Taro Maeyashiki)

This passage allows us to understand Twain's major shift in his view of Native Americans, as Tabei highlights. After this lecture, Twain was exposed to stories and legends about Indians while traveling along the Mississippi River in 1882 (300-301). Tabei highlights the possibility that

Twain, inspired by these Native American legends, came to consider the Native Americans from "multiple perspectives" (302).

Section 4: About Twain and the Aborigines

In "From White to Red," Tabei shows that Twain's view of Native Americans was influenced by his encounters with indigenous Australians (Tabei 325-326). From this point on, I will focus on a different section of Twain's book *Following the Equator*, in which he writes about Aborigines, from the one pointed out by Tabei. The following passages are considered important in interpreting Twain's view of Aborigines, so I will analyze them from the viewpoint of natural man.

Regarding the Aboriginal savages (*Following the Equator*, 1897)

Twain, who had been disgusted with the Native Americans since his first encounter with the Goshutes, was certainly given a new perspective when, 25 years after writing *Roughing It*, he saw the ability of the savage Aborigines to out-compete the white man. In *Following the Equator*, Twain describes the indigenous Aboriginal people in Australia.

[…] a literature might be made out of the aboriginal all by himself, his character and ways are so freckled with varieties—varieties not staled by familiarity, but new to us. You do not need to invent any picturesquenesses; whatever you want in that line he can furnish you; and they will not be fancies and doubtful, but realities and authentic. (*F. E.*[14] 176)

This is very different from the assessment he made of the Goshute people, who share a common identity as indigenous peoples. Twain's respect for Aboriginal people is also evident in the following quote:

In his history, as preserved by the white man's official records, he is everything—everything that a human creature can be. He covers the entire ground. He is a coward—there are a thousand fact to prove it. He is brave—there are a thousand facts to prove it. He is treacherous—oh, beyond imagination! he is faithful, loyal, true—the

---

[14]   *F.E.* is the abbreviation of *Following the Equator*

white man's records supply you with a harvest of instances of it that are noble, worshipful, and pathetically beautiful. (*F.E.* 177)

In Twain's view, the Aboriginal people contain the full spread of all human qualities. Twain highlights their shortcomings, but also praises their character.

He [Aboriginal people] knows all the great and many of the little constellations, and has names for them; he has a symbol-writing by means of which he can convey messages far and wide among the tribes; he has a correct eye for form and expression, and draws a good picture; he can track a fugitive by delicate traces which the white man's eye cannot discern, and by methods which the finest white intelligence cannot master; he makes a missile which science itself cannot duplicate without the model—if with it; a missile whose secret baffled and defeated the searchings and theorizings of the white mathematicians for seventy years; and by an art all his own he performs miracles with it which the white man cannot approach untaught, nor parallel after teaching. Within certain limits this savage's intellect is the alertest and the brightest known to history or tradition. (*F.E.* 177-178)

The above quote describes Aboriginal artistry and clearly shows Twain's admiration.

Fenimore Cooper lost his chance. He would have known how to value these people. He wouldn't have traded the dullest of them for the brightest Mohawk he ever invented.

All savages draw outline pictures upon bark; but the resemblances are not close, and expression is usually lacking. But the Australian aboriginal's pictures of animals were nicely accurate in form, attitude, carriage; and he put spirit into them, and expression. And his pictures of white people and natives were pretty nearly as good as his pictures of the other animals. (*F.E.* 180)

Twain assumes that if Fenimore Cooper had met the Aborigines, he would have known their value.

The aboriginal can make a fire by friction. I have tried that.

All savages are able to stand a good deal of physical pain. The Australian aboriginal has this quality in a well-developed degree. (*F.E.* 181)

It is clear that Twain revered the Aborigines. The skill of Aboriginal people in painting is definitely something that captured Twain's heart. It is quite possible that Twain's opinion of indigenous peoples changed after this travelog.

Section 5: Twain and Native Americans in the later years.

"Which was the Dream?" (1897)

I have decided to discuss "Which was the Dream?" (1897), a work not covered in Mr. Tabei's "From White to Red. "Which was the Dream?" has already been briefly explained in the *Mark Twain Literature/Cultural Encyclopedia* (Kamei 171), but I will examine it in more detail here.

The focus of the story is a white family. Bessie was a dreamer and philosopher, always thinking. She tried to understand the world around her from her own point of view, not from established values. One day Bessie tells her tutor about the Native Americans.

For some months, now, the governess has been instructing her about the American Indians. One day, a few weeks ago, Alice, with a smitten conscience, said–

[Alice] 'Potie, I have been so busy that I haven't been in at night, lately, to hear you say your prayers. Maybe I can come in tonight. Shall I?'

Bessie hesitated, waited for her thought to formulate itself, then brought it out–

[Bessie] 'Mamma. I don't play as much as I used to—and I don't pray in the same way. Maybe you would not be pleased with the way I pray now.'

[Alice] 'Tell me about it, Potie.'

[Bessie] 'Well, mamma, I don't know that I can make you understand. But you know, the Indians thought they were wrong. By and by maybe it will be found out that we are wrong, too. So now I only pray that there may be a God—and a heaven—or something better.' (*Mark Twain's Which Was the Dream and Other Symbolic Writings of the Later Years*, 49-50)

It is worth noting that Bessie's image of Native Americans, as created by Twain, radically undermines Twain's previous view of Native Americans: according to Bessie, both the Native Americans and the American people are at fault, and prayer is needed for both.

"Extract from Captain Stormfield's Visit to Heaven."

In the last years of his life, "Extract from Captain Stormfield's Visit to Heaven" depicts Native Americans, not whites, as the inhabitants of Heaven, and I would like to look back at that here.

[…] there was a lot of Injun tribes and they kept up such another war-whooping that they kind of took the tuck out of music. (Twain, *The Bible According to Mark Twain* 157)

Captain Stormfield encounters several Native Americans, but it is interesting to note his calm and objective observation that "war-whooping that they kind of took the tuck out of the music." As Tabei highlights, this shows that Twain, in his later years, once again regarded the Native Americans as his own kind. In addition, as Tabei points out, the captain's joy at meeting the Paiute Native Americans (Tabei 328) can be seen as a symbol of Twain's new view of Native Americans.

CHAPTER 2

THE NATIVE AMERICAN'S MESSAGE AND ITS ADVOCATE, TWAIN

Section 1: Desire for Freedom

We have already mentioned the incident in *Huck Finn and Tom Sawyer Among the Indians* in which almost an entire white family is killed. Tom's ideal image of Native Americans was destroyed by this incident. What was Tom's image of Native Americans before this incident? Here is a line from Tom that shows it conclusively.

> [Huck]: 'Tom, where did you learn about Injuns - how noble they was, and all that?'

> He [Tom] gave me a look that showed me I had hit him hard, very hard, and so I wished I hadn't said the words. He turned away his head, and after about a minute he said "Cooper's novels," and didn't say anything more, and I didn't say anything more, and so that changed subject. (*H.A.I* 50)

As Tabei has already highlighted regarding the above quote, this is a scene in which Tom experiences Twain's disillusionment with the Native Americans.

From a natural man perspective, the background of the Native Americans' violent behavior is that, deprived of their freedom due to the violation of their territory, the Native Americans sought a self-sufficient living environment and spiritual liberation from the bondage created by the intervention of the U.S. government.

Section 2: Imperialism

As already noted in *Huck Finn and Tom Sawyer Among the Indians*, Tabei points out that Twain has a white and Native American perspective. I have found a line in Brace's dialog that provides evidence for this, and I quote it below. In this scene, Peggy's fiancée, Blaise, speculates on how Peggy and her family were murdered by the Native Americans.

> 'I wonder what the nation put 'em on the war path. It was perfectly peaceable on the Plains a little while back, or I wouldn't a had the folks start, of course. And I wonder if it's *general* war, or only some little private thing.' (*H.A.I* 55)

Brace is a man who was engaged to the daughter of a white family known to Huck and says that such a murder of an entire white family would not have occurred not long ago. He points out that it could have been triggered by some kind of conflict or grudge. Brace then deepens his thoughts and says the following quote.

> [...] some white man has killed a relation of that Injun, and so he has hunted up some whites to retaliate on. (*H.A.I* 57)

In other words, he speculates that this is revenge for the killing by a white man of one of the Native Americans' relatives.

There is another short story by Twain, *Indiantown* (1899). This short story is included in Katsumi Satouchi's translation of Twain's book, *Which Was It?* In this story, there are Mr. and Mrs. Gridley, whose personalities contrast with each other. The husband, David Gridley, is a writer, and Mr. Satouchi describes his character as "extremely divided between his inner and outer worlds" (467). Satouchi argues that his wife Susan, who has a lofty temperament from the East, constantly monitors and warns David of his misbehavior (Satouchi 467). Satouchi notes that when David wrote a story about the cruelty of the Native Americans, Susan modified it and sent the Native Americans to Sunday school, a setting that was completely contrary to David's intentions (Satouchi 431). He then states the following:

> Gridley's relationship with his wife Susan is displaced by the relationship between the Indians and the white Americans who

capture and civilize them. [...] Reviewing this portrait of the wife-beater David Gridley, the possibility emerges that the story is not only Twain's "personal history," but also a "national history," in which nineteenth-century Native Americans were exterminated by whites, deprived of their original language, and tamed. (Satouchi 470)

This is the reality of U.S. imperialism.

Section 3: Pacifism and Egalitarianism

"Which was the Dream?" (1967)

We have already mentioned Bessie's words in "Section 5: Twain and the Native Americans in the Later Years," but let us examine them again here. She had the following to say about Native Americans:

> 'Well, mamma, I don't know that I can make you understand. But you know, the Indians thought they were wrong. By and by maybe it will be found out that we are wrong, too. So now I only pray that there may be a God—and a heaven—or something better.' (*H.A. I* 56)

In his autobiography, Twain describes this passage as follows:

> I wrote down this pathetic prayer in its precise wording, at the time, in a record which we kept of the children's sayings, and my reverence for it has grown with the years that have passed over my head since then. Its untaught grace and simplicity are a child's, but the wisdom and the pathos of it are of all the ages that have come and gone since the race of man has lived, and longed, and hoped, and feared, and doubted. (Twain, *Autobiography of Mark Twain, Volume 1*, 326)

Twain appreciates "the wisdom and the pathos" of Bessie's wish, an innocent 8-year-old girl encapsulating all the tribulations of the times in which man has lived. Twain's view of Native Americans changed drastically when he wrote this work. In this work, we can see the values of Rousseau's natural man, "pacifism" and "egalitarianism," in which whites and Native Americans are equal.

Native Americans in Heaven: "Extract from Captain Stormfield's Visit to Heaven" (1909)

In "Mark Twain's Masterpieces of Humor," Yoko Arima explains that "Extract from Captain Stormfield's Visit to Heaven," published in 1907, was only part of the original (chapters 3 and 4), with the remaining chapters 1, 2, 5, and 6 published only in 1970 (256). The Japanese translation of the book included only chapters 3 and 4, and it was not until Arima's translation of the remaining chapters that they were included in "Mark Twain's Masterpieces of Humor" (256). Arima describes the contents of the first chapter as follows:

> First, by reading chapters 1 and 2, you will learn about the scene where the captain draws his last breath and about his experiences during the 30 years of flight since his death and what he experienced along the way. The story is quite elaborate and describes how the captain, who had lost the loneliness of flying alone in the dark and the sense of racism peculiar to white people, flew at very high speed with Jews and black people as his guide. (Arima 256)

I searched the original text for the passage indicated by the above quote and came across it, quoted below.

> I [Captain Stormfield] was born sociable, and never could stand solitude. I was trained to a prejudice against Jews—Christians always are, you know - ut such of it would have disappeared then, I was so lonesome and so anxious for company. (Twain, *The Bible According to Mark Twain* 142)

In his last work, "Extract from Captain Stormfield's Heaven," Tabei said Twain dispelled his prejudiced stereotypes by making Native Americans the inhabitants of heaven and reconsidered and revised his view of Native Americans (336).

> In a previous study, John Kucich made the following observations:

> By the time he drafted Captain Stormfield, Twain's quarrel with James Fenimore Cooper had cooled, though some Indian-hating rhetoric survives in Sandy McWilliams's words to Stormfield. When advising

the captain on where to settle in heaven, he says, "You see what the Jersey district of heaven is for whites; well, the California district is thousand times worse. It swarms with a mean kind of leather-headed mud-colored angels—Digger mainly - and your nearest neighbor is likely to be a million miles away" (175). Yet Sandy's account is countered to some degree by Stormfield's fond reunion at heaven's gate with the Pai Ute he knew from his own California days, a "mighty good fellow" and a member of the tribe to which the so-called "Diggers" also belonged. (Kucich 88)

It is important to note that Twain's image of the Native American was eventually transformed into Rousseau's peaceful, egalitarian natural man.

Section 4: The Suppressed History of Native Americans

Before white settlement, Native Americans did not "own" land, but rather shared it. However, the settlers changed their values and conception of interest in the land, and the land became a source of territorial disputes for the Native Americans. Takako Takeda points out in "The Establishment of the Twain Brand" that there is "a record of the confiscation of 110 million acres of land from the Indians in 1871" (15). The Native Americans tribes were fighting each other because they were running out of food and faced life-or-death problems. These problems would have been less likely if settlement had not occurred. We will try to get a general idea of how the Native Americans lived before the white invasion by quoting from the *Encyclopedia of the History of the European Invasion of the Indians* edited by Jeffrey Schultz:

When Europeans first colonized North America, they repeatedly recorded the generosity of the continent's indigenous peoples. Generally, Europeans were welcomed and were provided a place to build their towns. The cultures of Europe and North America, however, had—and have—very different understandings about the land and its control. Most native nations have always had some way to determine who could use various lands and resources. However, they did not share the European idea that a person could have the right to control land to the extent of using up whatever resources it contained. Native-American resource was designed to be sustainable over the long term. (Schultz 648)

Native American resources were treated carefully so that they could be preserved for a long time. These differences in values are thought to have been the genesis of the struggle between the Native Americans and the colonists. What was the Native American conception of land?

Native North Americans conceived themselves and the land to be part of a living and sacred system. This system was based on reciprocity, meaning people who occupy the land are supposed to give something back to it in exchange for the use of its resources. When the United States was formed, it continued the practice begun by the European colonial nations of making treaties with native nations. The treaties usually "reserved" certain lands, "reservations " for Native-American use. The battles fought for control of the continent were generally of two types: Native-American attempts to protect their remaining resources, which resulted in pitched battles, and efforts by non-Indians to exterminate entire villages, which took the form of one-sided massacres.

While modern conflicts over land and resources seldom break into the violence, there is still constant conflict among Indians and non-Indians surrounding these issues. (Schultz 648)

As Greg Velm says on this matter, "American Indians fought desperate wars among themselves for the few resources left." (Velm 71) The U.S. took steps to stop the struggles with the Native American tribes that settlement brought about, but the situation did not improve much. How did the U.S. territorial expansion change the lives of Native Americans, as discussed in the encyclopedia edited by Spencer C. Tucker?

The expansion of the United States from sea to sea unleashed a great migration of Americans across the Indian territory of the Great Plains. Subsequently, the U.S. government focused on how to dissuade the Indians from attacking the migrants. Signed at Fort Laramie in Wyoming Territory in 1851, the Treaty of Fort Laramie treaty attempted to establish relations with seven northern Plains Indian tribes, including the Sioux, and secure their promise not to interfere with American overland migrants, roads, forts, and trading posts. (Tucker ed.1134)

This was a convenient policy for the U.S. government to pursue its national project. Was the U.S. government's concern about American Native Americans justified? We will continue to examine these details in the encyclopedia edited by Tucker.

At the same time, the treaty specified the territories assigned to the seven tribes and exacted a promise that they would not fight among themselves. In return, the United States was to protect the Indians from harm by Americans and to provide financial and material assistance to the Indians for the purpose of taking up agriculture. The government was pursuing a policy of trying to integrate the Indians into American society by giving them incentives to adopt American ways. (Tucker ed. 1134)

While this assimilation policy may have been designed to protect the Native Americans, there is no doubt that U.S. national interest was paramount. How did the Native Americans lose their homes?

The U.S. government signed another Treaty of Fort Laramie in 1868, also with the Sioux and allied tribes. This second treaty established for the Sioux an extensive reservation in present-day South Dakota, but the peace was similarly short-lived. Just eight years later war with the Sioux broke out due in no small part to the discovery of gold deposits in the Black Hills of South Dakota. (Tucker ed. 1134)

The Native Americans had lived on a mutualistic basis and had no desire to harm others before settlement. However, the invasion of whites made life difficult for them. There can be no more severe ordeal, both mentally and physically, than encroachment on one's living space. In fact, Yuko Yamamoto, in "Mark Twain's Unfinished Work: *Huck Finn and Tom Sawyer Among the Indians*: A Journey into Memory and Deep Psychology," identifies the Native Americans in *Huck Finn and Tom Sawyer Among the Indians* as this Sioux tribe (178). If those Indians were Sioux, as Yamamoto says, the presumption of revenge for the white man's slaughter would be supported.

Section 5: Characteristics and Environment of Native Americans as Natural Man (*Huck Finn and Tom Sawyer Among the Indians*) (*1889*)

Why are Native Americans the perfect natural man in *Huck Finn and Tom Sawyer Among the Indians*? First, we need to know about the environment in which the Native Americans live. There is a scene in which Huck and his party reach Indian territory and immediately enjoy the beauty of nature.

> By and by we struck level country, and a pretty smooth path, and not so much woods, and the moonlight was perfectly splendid, and so was the stillness. You couldn't hear nothing but the creaking [creaking] of the saddles. After a while there was that cool and fresh feeling that tells you day is coming; and then the sun come up behind us, and made the leaves and grass and flowers shine and sparkle, on account of the dew, and the birds let go and begun to sing like everything. (*HAI* 39)

The scene above is the first day of their journey. The story goes on:

> So then we took to the woods, and made camp, and picketed the mules, and laid off and slept a good deal of the day. Three more nights we traveled that way, and laid up daytimes, and everything was mighty pleasant. We never run across anybody, and hardly ever see a light. After that, we judged we was so far from home that we was safe; so then we begun to travel by daylight. (*HAI* 39)

The view unfolding before Huck and the others as they travel deeper into Indian territory, now by daylight, is as follows.

> It was just the place for a camp; the likeliest we had found yet. Big stream of water, and considerable many trees along it. The rest of the country, as far as you could see, any which-way you looked, clear to where the sky touched the earth, was just long levels and low waves like what I reckon the ocean would be, if the ocean was made out of grass. Away off, miles and miles, was one tree standing by itself, and away off the other way was another, and here and yonder another

and another scattered around; and the air was so clear you would think they was close by, but it warn's so, most of them was miles away. (*HAI* 42)

Let us explore the natural man element of the Indians who appear here.

(i) Survival techniques

Tom strongly urges Huck and Jim to go to the Indian Territory, but they are satisfied with the status quo and are not very enthusiastic. Tom then emphasizes how wonderful the Native Americans are:

[...] and if he sees one single blade of grass bent down, it's all he wants, he knows which way to go to find the enemy that done it, and he can read all kinds of trifling little signs just the same way with his eagle eye which you wouldn't ever see at all, and if he sees a little whiff of smoke going up in the air thirty-five miles off, he knows in a second if it's a friend's camp fire or an enemy's, just by the smell of the smoke, because they're the most giftedest people in the whole world [...]. (*HFA* 36-37)

Here, Native Americans have a survival technique unique to natural man, with an eye for tiny details that normal humans overlook.

(ii) Simple desires

The following quote suggests that Native Americans maintain as simple a lifestyle as possible. "They were naked from the waist up" (43), Huck explains. From this, we can understand that the Native Americans wear almost nothing. This shows that Native Americans have little or no desire for material goods.

(iii) Desire for freedom

I have already discussed the desire for freedom in Chapter 2 (Section 1) of Part 3, so I will omit it.

(iv) Heretical beliefs

Native Americans are polytheistic pagans. Tom says the following about Native American deaths: "They sing when they're dying." (36) Brace, meanwhile, is familiar with Indian beliefs and describes the Native American religion as follows:

> Injuns hadn't only but two Gods, a good one and a bad one, and they never paid no attention to the good one, nor ever prayed to him or worried about him at all, but only tried their level best to flatter up the bad god and keep on the good side of him; because the good one loved them and wouldn't ever think of doing them any harm and so there warn't any occasion to be bothering him with prayers and things, because he was always doing the very best he could for them anyway, and prayers couldn't better it; but all the trouble come from the bad god, who was setting up nights to think up ways to bring them bad luck and bust up all their plans, and never fooled away a chance to do them all the harm he could; and so the sensible thing was to keep praying and fussing around him all the time, and get him to let up. Brace thought more of the Great Spirit than he did of his own mother, but he never fretted about him. He said his mother wouldn't hurt him, would she? — well then, the Great Spirit wouldn't, that was sure. (*HFA* 61-62)

(vii) Compassion

Native Americans have a generous spirit. Tom portrays them as follows:

> They're just all generous and unstingeableness. (*HFA* 36)

This means that Native Americans are not mean-spirited. They are friendly to others.

(viii) Egalitarianism

The next scene shows Huck and his group meeting and being welcomed by an Native American tribe.

> They set around our fire till bedtime, the first night, and took supper with us, and passed around the pipe, and was very friendly, and made signs to us, and grunted back, when we signed anything they understood, and pretty much everything they see that they liked, they wanted it. (*HFA* 43)

As can be seen from the above quote, the Native Americans are idyllic natural men, having dinner with Huck and the others and trying to communicate in a friendly manner.

Section 6: Twain and Native American Religion in Later Years

Twain was in his twenties when he was in Nevada, and as already mentioned, he had a dislike for Native Americans. However, about 25 years later, when he was in his fifties, Twain's opinion had changed.

> 'We have to keep our God placated with prayers and even then we are never sure of him—how much higher and finer is the Indian's God.' (Philipps 308)

As we have discussed, the evolution of Twain's view of Native Americans affected the content of his work. Although Twain was disillusioned with Native Americans, he changed his opinions of them through exposure to their art forms, and by tracing their history. In fact, other factors may have influenced Twain's view of Native Americans. Specific examples are his encounter with indigenous Aborigines as recounted by Tabei and his feelings towards Philippine natives[15]. These are discussed in detail in the "Notes" section. In his novels, Twain depicts

---

[15] In fact, Twain had a global worldview: war broke out between the Philippines and the U.S. in 1899 and lasted to 1902. The following quote shows that Twain criticized U.S. actions as imperialistic and took a defensive position against the natives of the Philippines.

The Philippine-American War would drag on for another year, with sporadic uprising and fighting lasting until 1906. Mark Twain continued to follow the Philippine situation closely, and kept up a stream of commentary, even though friends advised that he might be jeopardizing his livelihood, given the wide public support for the war and occupation. (Kolb 313)

After the capture of Aguinaldo, the Philippine-American War more or less quieted down, but Mark Twain continued to advocate independence for the islands, which did not come until 1946. He kept his pen sharpened for other causes as well, and persisted in opposing exploitation of native peoples. (Kolb 315)

After the capture of Aguinaldo, the first president of the Republic of the Philippines, the momentum of the Philippine–American War waned, but Twain still supported Philippine independence. According to Sharon Delmendo, he is credited with pointing out the slaughter of Filipino natives by American soldiers:

Native Americans as natural men, whose senses are superior to those of ordinary people, and who live in harmony with nature by skillfully using it. The Native Americans described by Twain in *Huck Finn and Tom Sawyer Among the Indians* also had an idyllic life before the invasion by the white man. If their lives had not been destroyed by the white man's ambition to settle in the West, they would not have been put in such a difficult position, nor become as violent. One of the messages of the Native Americans may be an indictment of the U.S. government for the disgrace and wastefulness of its pioneering policies, a message that a more productive and rational outcome might have been produced if they had sought a path of coexistence with the Native Americans as natural men.[16]

> [...] as Mark Twain pointed out, some estimated that 30,000 American soldiers killed 1 million Filipino natives during the Philippine-American War (Rieder150)

Whether this attitude of Twain toward the natives led to a change in his view of the Native Americans is not certain, but we think it is a factor that is sufficiently worth speculating upon.

[16] According to Arima, one of the manuscripts of *The Mysterious Stranger Manuscripts*, published in 1969, was actually written by Twain between 1897 and 1900 (Kamei 111)

PART 4

NATURAL MAN-LIKE CHARACTER MESSAGES AND TWAIN'S CHANGING RELIGIOUS VIEWS

The characters of natural man have not only a natural element but also a message to send out to the world. While the characters we have analyzed so far have not been vocal, their messages implied in the work is clear. While we have dealt with human characters up to this point, we will now discuss Satan, a mysterious demon. We will also examine the relationship between religion and Satan as well as the other natural man-like characters we have discussed, and we will decipher the message of each character.

CHAPTER 1

SATAN IN CONTACT WITH NATURAL MAN

We have discussed the history of natural man in Part I, analyzed natural man-like characters in Part II, and unraveled Twain's view of Native Americans and the Native American message in Part III. The characters discussed so far are relatively easy to imagine as natural man as described by Rousseau. However, this will be challenged when we consider Satan. This natural man-like character has the basic characteristics of a natural man, such as survival skills and a desire for freedom, but he is not of this world. It is an existence reminiscent of a supernatural universe.

Section 1: *The Chronicle of Young Satan* (1969)

Section 1: Twain and Satan

In Twain's works, natural man-like characters such as Huck and Jim appear. However, there are also those who have supernatural abilities, such as Satan, who has similarities with natural man. In *The Letters of Mark Twain, Twain* writes:

> From A.D. 350 to A.D. 1850 these gentlemen [Jesus and Satan] exercised a vaster influence over a fifth part of the human race by all other influences combined. Ninety-nine hundredths of this influence proceeded from Satan, the remaining fraction of it from Jesus. (*The Letters of Mark Twain* 169)

Previous research has shown that Twain read extrabiblical texts regarding Satan. Extrabiblical books are "Christian documents that are

close to and important but distinct from the canonical books of the Bible"
(Matsumura 421, cited and translated by Taro Maeyashiki). According to
Terry R. Wright:

> Twain apparently encountered an 1820 edition of *The Apocryphal New
> Testament* in a New York Library in 1867. (Wright 49)

According to Budd's *On Mark Twain,* he was also influenced by other
Satan-related works such as *Faust* and Voltaire's *Zadig* (150). Although
many references to Satan are found in the Bible, Steven C Weisenburger
has pointed out that the Satan in Twain's work is similar to the Satan of
extrabiblical sources. Extrabiblical books are quite different from the
ordinary Bible.

> [...] there is also an apocryphal Gospel of Thomas, commonly referred
> to as the "Infancy Story" of Jesus. It exists in four recensions, one
> each in Greek and Latin, two in Syriac. In it are narratives of Jesus's
> boyhood from his fifth to his twelfth years, narratives abounding
> with miracles: Jesus restores the dead to life, inflicts death on some
> who thwart his will, and makes birds out of clay (like Satan in Mark
> Twain's *Mysterious Stranger*)causes them to fly. (Weisenburger 282)

According to Weisenburger, there is an extrabiblical book called
"The Gospel of Thomas"[17] in which Jesus says that he can create birds
out of clay, a technique that is similar to the creation of birds out of clay
in Twain's *The Chronicle of Young Satan*. Now, let me show you the relevant
passage.

> He made birds out of clay and set them free and they flew away
> singing. At last I made bold to ask him to tell us who he was. "An
> angel," he said, quite simply, and set another clay bird free and
> clapped his hands and made it fly away. (*C.Y.S.*[18] *The Mysterious Stranger
> Manuscript* 47)

---

[17] One of the external books of the New Testament. A collection of sayings of Jesus,
supposedly written by his disciple Thomas. [...] It was included in a Coptic Gnostic
document discovered in Nag-Hamadi, Egypt, in 1945 (Matsumura 1846, cited and
translated by Taro Maeyashiki). This extrabiblical text is also considered heretical.
(Mounce 117)

[18] Abbreviation for *The Chronicle of Young Satan.*

In the above quote, Satan, as Weisenburger highlights, created birds out of clay and set them free in the sky. When Theodor Fischer, the protagonist, asked the devil who he was, Satan said "an angel".

So where in the Gospel of Thomas do we actually find such episodes? My research led me to L.W. Hurtado, who found two episodes of making birds out of clay in texts at the Orthodox Gregoriu Monastery. According to this prior research, Twain's references to Satan are the Gospel of Thomas and the Koran.

> [...] the multiple later copies of this infancy gospel, and its translation into a number of ancient languages, surely show that it came to be read in various Christian circles. Gero (1971:48-56) discusses versions in Greek, Latin, Syriac, Arabic, Armenian, Georgian, Ethiopic, and Old Church Slavonic. As he (Gero 1971:75) notes, 'Apparently, both Greek and Slavonic versions of apocryphal gospels were quite generally used in Orthodox monasteries as devotional reading.' Moreover, to judge by the references to Jesus in the Qur'an as 'he who made clay birds fly' (Surah 3.49, 5.110; one of the famous stories in the *Infancy Gospel of Thomas* 2.1-7) (Hurtado 158)

What is the content of these references? Let us begin with the passage presented in the Gospel of Thomas.

> This child Jesus, when five years old, was playing in the ford of a mountain stream; and He collected the flowing waters into pools, and made them clear immediately, and by a word alone He made them obey Him. And having made some soft clay, He fashioned out of it twelve sparrows. And it was the Sabbath when He did these things. (Robert 78)

Now, let us look at the passage in the Koran related to Twain's Satan that Hurtado focused on.

> In sura 3:49 the infant who prophesies his future work says he will make a bird model from clay, breathe on it, and it will become a real bird. The prediction is confirmed by the divine review of his life's work in sura 5:110; "you create a clay model of a bird by my permission." While references to Jesus healing lepers, giving sight

to the blind, and raising the dead in the same texts confirm the testimony of the gospels, this transformation of a clay model into a living bird is different type of story from the miracle stories found there. (Beaumont 4)

There are other similar descriptions in another version of the Gospel of Thomas. In fact, there are multiple versions of the Gospel of Thomas, which are compiled in different ways. These quotations are such:

The birds in the air are not seeking consciousness; they are the creation and evolution of God's unconditional love. They do not possess free will but are the will of God continuously expressing itself. They are God becoming, and have no sense of "separation" from God, whereas we may create the space of separation in choosing not to believe in God and in God's unconditional love. (Chesbro 21)

This quote is taken from *The Gospel of Thomas: A Spiritual Interpretation for the Aquarian Age*, edited by Chesbro. According to the Gospel of Thomas, a bird is a search for "consciousness". Birds are creatures of God's absolute love. Birds do not have free will, but God's will is always evident. They are living copies of God and do not want to be separated from Him. They have the right to choose whether or not to believe in God's absolute love. This means that Twain's boy Satan has set the bird free, and he has freed the bird from God's bondage. This would differ from the Christian worldview that obeying God is the way to freedom. The message that can be read from this extrabiblical scripture and the Koran is that by being free from God, one can be free from bondage and free spiritually and physically. Mark Twain's depiction of Satan's bird made of clay (Adam and Eve are also said to have been created from clay) illustrates the importance of being free from God through the act of setting the bird free.

Some critics also identify Twain's extrabiblical sources.

All is not reverential, then, for even the persona of the Reverend Mark Twain suggests sacred parody. Twain includes burlesque of the Christ story when discussing the Apocryphal New Testament in *The Innocents Abroad*. He provides extracts based upon his Alta California letter of June 2, 1867, in which he describes "a curious book" he had seen at a New York library, William Hone's edition of the Apocryphal New Testament(MYMB 251). Twain selectively includes extracts in his description, as Guy Caldwell suggests, "for comic emphasis" (1012). Working under the guise of simply providing information, Twain carefully places the burden for the burlesque on the "curious book" itself. All the while, Twain creates a comical interplay between the New Testament and the Apocryphal New Testament and between what he says and does not say. (Fulton 90)

According to Fulton, Twain actually picked up and read the extra-biblical books compiled by William Hone.[19] I have examined Satan's

---

[19] Excerpts from Hone's compilation of extrabiblical texts:

O prince Satan, though great keeper of the infernal regions, all thy advantages which though didst acquire by the forbidden tree, and the loss of Paradise, thou hast now lost by the wood of cross. (Hone 66)

O Satan, prince of all evil, author of death, and source of all pride, though shouldest first have inquired into the evil crimes of Jesus of Nazareth, and then though wouldest have found that he was guilty of no fault worthy of death. (Hone 66)

CHAP.VI.

Mary looks on a woman in whom Satan had taken up his abode, and she becomes dispossessed. Christ kissed by a bride made dumb by sorcerers, cures her, miraculously cures a gentle woman in whom Satan had taken up his abode. A leprous girl cured by the water in which he was washed, and becomes the servant of Joseph and Mary. The leprous son of a prince's wife cured in like manner.

Then they went into another city, where there was a woman possessed with devil, and in whom Satan, that cursed rebel, had taken up his abode. One night, when she went to fetch water, she could neither endure clothes on, nor to be in any house; but as often as they tied her with chains or cords, she brake them, and went out into desert places, and sometimes standing where rods crossed, and in church-yards, would throw stones at men. When St. Mary saw this woman, she pitied her; whereupon Satan presently left her, and fled away in the form of a young man, saying, Wo to me, because of thee, Mary, and thy son. (Hone 25)

CHAP.XIII.

A girl, whose blood Satan sucked, receives one of Christ's swaddling clothes from the Virgin, Satan comes like a dragon, and she shews it to him; flames and burning coals proceed from it and fall upon him; he is miraculously discomfited and leaves the girl. (Hone 33)

descriptions in these extra-biblical books, and they do not necessarily agree with Twain's Satan. However, they certainly provided material for Twain's image of Satan, and the details are explained in the notes.

It is conceivable that Twain created the works in which Satan appears with this knowledge of the Gospel of Thomas. Twain probably intermingled the formal New Testament with the extrabiblical New Testament in his writing with a sense of humor.

We now take a closer look at the main focus of this chapter, Twain's work, *The Mysterious Stranger*, also known as *The Chronicle of Young Satan*.

The *Chronicle of Young Satan is* set in the Austrian village of Eseldorf during the Middle Ages. The main characters are three young boys, including the narrator, Father Adolf, and his niece Marget. One day, the three boys encounter Satan while playing. When the boys learn of Satan's true identity, they are awe-struck, but his friendly and innocent attitude attracts them, and they become friends. Later, Satan uses various types of magic to cause miracles and disasters, and changes the destinies of the villagers.

"Eseldorf was a paradise for us boys"

Illustration by N. C. Wyeth (in Public Domain)

Section 2: Satan's Similarities to Natural Man

The message of Satan as portrayed by Twain is similar to the message of Rousseau's criticism of civilization through natural man. Now, let us list Satan's natural man traits in concrete terms.

(i) Survival techniques

Satan is immortal and does not need to use survival techniques. This supernatural Satan can conjure up natural disasters at will. The following quote illustrates this.

> Satan said we would have a storm, now, and an earthquake, if we liked, but we must stand off a piece, out of danger. (*C.Y.S.* in *The Mysterious Stranger Manuscript* 51)

Shortly after the above quote, he does indeed call up a storm over the miniature castle and 500 tiny people within it he had created and animated by his supernatural power.

> A small storm-cloud began to settle down black over the castle, and the miniature lightning and thunder began to play and the ground to quiver and the wind to pipe and wheeze and the rain to fall, and all the people flocked into the castle for shelter. The cloud settled down blacker and blacker and one could see the castle only dimly through it; the lightnings blazed out flash upon flash and they pierced the castle and set it on fire and the flames shone out red and fierce through the cloud [...]. (*C.Y.S.* 51-52)

In terms of governing nature, one does not need to be equipped with survival skills with this kind of power. However, Satan's choice to cause natural disasters shows the depth of his connection with nature.

(ii) Desire for freedom

The following sentence shows that Satan can act out of his own free will, unbound and uninfluenced by anyone. Satan "created birds of clay and set them free, and they flew away chirping" (*C.Y.S.* 18). Satan's willingness to free the birds without killing them links to natural man's desire for freedom.

(iii) Heretical beliefs

The first pagan behavior of Satan is respect for rattlesnakes. In one scene, a daughter named Lilly falls in love with Satan at first sight and tells her mother about it. Lilly describes Satan as follows: "He is ever so kind-hearted, mother, and admires rattlesnakes" (*C.Y.S.* 71).

While showing Theodor India, Satan also changes himself into a local to perform a miracle with a juggler. He "impersonated a native and wrapped himself in a turban and loincloth" (145-146). Most Native Americans are, of course, polytheistic.

(v) Animal friendship

Animals come close to Satan and climb up his body. To the animals, Satan is like a friend.

> The wild creatures trooped in from everywhere, and climbed all over Satan, and sat on his shoulder and his head, and rummaged his pockets, and made themselves at home-squirrels, rabbits, snakes, birds, butterflies, every creature you could name; and the rest would sit around in a crowd and look at him and admire him and worship him and chatter and squawk and talk and laugh, and he would answer back in their own languages. (*C.Y.S.*, *Mysterious Stranger* 117)

This reveals the intimacy between Satan and the animals.

(vi) Innocence (conscience rooted in nature)

Regarding natural man's innocence, it is innocence for the lack of morality.

> No, the Fall did not affect me nor the rest of the relationship. It was only he that I was named for who ate of the fruit of the tree and then beguiled the man and the woman with it. We [Satan and the rest] others are still ignorant of sin; we are not able to commit it; we are without blemish, and shall abide in that estate always. (*C.Y.S.*, *Mysterious Stranger* 49)

Satan inherited the name Satan from his uncle, and he insists that his uncle alone is responsible for the fall of Adam and Eve, and that he and the rest of his relatives are completely blameless. Satan says the same thing about animals that have no morality.

No brute ever does a cruel thing—that is the monopoly of the snob with the Moral Sense. When a brute inflicts pain he does it innocently; it is not wrong; for him there is no such thing as wrong. And he does not inflict pain for the pleasure of inflicting it—only man does that. Inspired by that mongrel Moral Sense of his! A Sense whose function is to distinguish between right and wrong, with liberty to choose which of them he will do. Now what advantage can he get out of that? He is always choosing, and in nine cases out of ten he prefers the wrong. There shouldn't be any wrong; and without the Moral Sense there couldn't be any. And yet he is such an unreasoning creature that he is not able to perceive that the Moral Sense degrades him to the bottom layer of animated beings and is a shameful possession. (*C.Y.S.*, *The Mysterious Stranger Manuscripts* 44-45)

The inability to judge right from wrong is evidence of innocence. Satan's "moral sense" has been discussed by Yukiko Asahi in her article "Mark Twain's Satan".

Mark Twain's Satan assumes the role of thoroughly denouncing the human conscience or "moral sense." [Twain] has Satan served as an agent to expose man's self-deception that he is the most superior being in creation because he possesses a "moral sense". (Asahi 115-116, cited and translated by Taro Maeyashiki)

In the following quote, Satan explains how civilization has turned man to killing.

It is a remarkable progress. In five or six thousand years five or six high civilizations have risen, flourished, commanded the wonder of the world, then faded out and disappeared; and not one of them except the latest, ever invented any sweeping and adequate way to kill people. They all did their best, to kill being the chiefest but only the Christian Civilization has scored a triumph to be proud of. (*C.Y.S.*, *The Mysterious Stranger Manuscripts* 137)

He condemns Christian civilization as the most sinful of murderers. In other words, Satan is clearly ridiculing and satirizing civilization. This criticism of civilization is also consistent with the views of Twain and Rousseau.

In this chapter, we have discussed Satan, a being beyond human knowledge, and therefore, although he is not a human being, he is a natural man-like character. As I have already mentioned, Satan's ability to cause natural disasters is a sure sign that he has a deep connection with the natural world. In addition, his rapport with animals is a good match for Joan. The fact that he regards animals and natural man as if they were his relatives also indicates the close relationship between Satan and nature.

What is Satan's message? It is "natural man, savage," whom Satan respects. He reveres the natural man, who has only simple desires in the natural environment, the opposite of civilization, and has no civilized elements such as morality. He also denounces the folly of civilization. One can also take the view that all genocides in human history were brought about by civilization, and that it is important to return to nature if only to purify the taint of it. One may also argue that we should scrutinize the negative legacy of civilization from a primitive perspective, learn from history, and restore the products of nature that people have lost sight of.

CHAPTER 2

NATURAL MAN-LIKE CHARACTER AND RELIGION

Religion is significant to Twain's natural man character. Although Huck had always distrusted Christianity, he was aware of the difference between heaven and hell. Huck knew that by rescuing Jim, a African American runaway slave, he would be disobeying the law. He also knew that to disobey the law was to disobey the teachings of Christianity because at that time, the church was interpreting the Bible to suit white people and justifying their attempts to enslave African American people. The loss of slaves as property was as serious as the loss of funds, and the owners were entitled to recover their lost property. Huck was determined to go to hell and save Jim, but inwardly, he was also afraid of going there.

Joan of Arc was a Catholic who was also familiar with the spirits of the forest, and her criticism of the Christian version of Satan, a natural man-like being, also has Christianity at its core.

I will now examine the religion of Mark Twain's natural man character and discuss the evolution of his religious views.

Section 1: *Adventures of Huckleberry Finn* (1884)

Let's take *Adventures of Huckleberry Finn* first. Jim has been sold to others by crooks. Huck realizes that the only way to save Jim is to inform his owner, Mrs. Watson, of the situation and ask her to take him back. Huck tries to write a letter about it but agonizes over whether it is really a good idea to have Mrs. Watson come and pick up Jim.

> I [Huck] was the best friend old Jim ever had in the world, and the only one he's got now; and then I happened to look around, and see that paper.
>
> It was a close place. I took it up, and held it in my hand. I was a-trembling, because I'd got to decide, forever, betwixt two things, and I knowed it. I studied a minute, sort of holding my breath, and then says to myself:
>
> 'All right, then, I'll go to hell' —and tore it up.
>
> It was awful thoughts and awful words, but they was said. And I let them stay said; and never thought no more about reforming. (*H.F.* 223)

In the end, Huck decides that he will not give Jim to anyone else, even if he has to go to hell, and that he will rescue him himself. Huck was aware of how inconsistent the idea of going to hell was with Christian beliefs, but he did not reconsider his decision.

Section 2: *Personal Recollections of Joan of Arc* (1896)

Joan of Arc believed in the Christian God, and the forest nymphs were her beloved companions. The following quote shows that the mixing of nature and religion was common in those days.

> Paganism before Christianity was a Celtic belief in nature itself; the mysterious and the uncanny are the elements that convince us of the unfathomable power of the great outdoors. (Deguchi et al. 205, cited and translated by Taro Maeyashiki)

It is significant that Mark Twain gifted Joan with this unique religious view. The fact that Twain's portrayal of Joan of Arc as a heretic was always positive is also evidence of the richness of his religious views. What was Twain's message through Joan's death? We will read about the fate of Joan of Arc, who was destroyed by Christianity, nature worship, and faith.

Section 1: Joan of Arc's Natural Man Element

It is interesting how Joan's natural man element was seen by the British, who found it convenient evidence of Joan's heretic status, since Domrémy, where Joan was born and raised, believed in a mixed religion of spiritism and Christianity. These quotes are from *The God of the Witches* by Margaret Murray, an archeologist and folklorist, about heretical beliefs in Joan's Lorraine region.

> She came from Lorraine, a district where a century earlier the Synod of Trèves had fulminated against 'all kinds of magic, sorcery, witchcraft, auguries, superstitious writings, observing of days and months, prognostics drawn from the flight of birds or similar things, observation of the stars in order to judge of the destiny of persons born under certain constellations, the illusions of women who boast that they ride at night with Diana or with Herodias and a multitude of other women.' (Murray 177)

Originally, the existence of fairies and dragons was familiar to people in the Middle Ages. In China, India, Southeast Asia, Mesopotamia, and Egypt, where agriculture flourished, dragons were thought of as "nature gods" (Sugisaki 127) in prehistoric times. In medieval Europe, however, dragons were generally regarded as incarnations of evil. However, the custom of believing in dragons as "protectors of cities" still exists in northern France and Belgium (Gueusquin, translated by Higuchi, 123).

The people of the village of Domrémy, as portrayed by Mark Twain, seemed to believe in legends about dragons, even though they were Christians. A dragon also appears in the Bible's Revelation of John, where it is identified as Satan, and the possibility of a Christian connection cannot be denied. They also believed in the existence of fairies at the same time. In Christianity, fairies were also regarded as demons. Next, let us look at Twain's description of dragons.

> [...] in still earlier times prodigious dragons that spouted fire and poisonous vapours from their nostrils had their homes in there. In fact, one was still living in there in our own time. It was as long as a tree, and had a body as big around as a tierce, and scales like

overlapping great tiles, and deep ruby eyes as large as a cavalier's hat, and an anchor-fluke on its tail as big as I don't know what, but very big, even unusually so for a dragon, as everybody said who knew about dragons. It was thought that this dragon was of a brilliant blue colour, with gold mottlings, but no one had ever seen it, therefore this was not known to be so, it was only an opinion.' (*J.A.* 20)

These are not portrayals that can be described as demonic. If anything, the representations of dragons here express the awe and reverence of the people.

How was Joan's fusion of Christianity and nature beliefs, as a natural man-like being, interpreted by the British? For the British, defining Joan as a heretic was a convenient interpretation. As Twain emphasizes, the British conducted a meticulous study of Joan's background, etc., and the dominant view of her natural man element became was as pagan and incompatible with Christianity.

First, the Church cited Joan's interaction with fairies as a reason for condemning her heretical beliefs. Fairies were interpreted by Christians as being equivalent to evil spirits.

As a child she had loved the fairies, she had spoken a pitying word for them when they were banished from their home, she had played under their tree and around their fountain —hence she was a comrade of evil spirits. (*J.A.* 379)

The possibility of "self-worship" was also raised when Joan placed a garland on the fairy tree Bourlemont, which they suggested had been done to honor the spirits. The fact that she was worshiped rather than respected by the people caused her to be seen as a heretic (Twain 366).

Joan was also regarded as a witch-like being who practiced demonic worship.

[…] a sorceress, a false prophet, an invoker and companion of evil spirits, a dealer in magic, a person ignorant of the Catholic faith, a schismatic; she is sacrilegious, an idolater, an apostate, a blasphemer of God and His saints […]. (*J.A.* 378)

The judges believed that the "voice" she claimed to have first heard at the age of 13 was not the voice of an angel, etc.; Joan's accomplishments and her act of wearing men's clothing were considered connected to the devil. (J.A. 341-342).

The focus was on whether Joan had committed other heretical acts and on the issue of the veneration of saints such as St. Catherine and St. Marguerite (Twain 427), and whether people kissing Joan was Joan worship (45). Some also suggested that because Joan knew the exact location of the sword, which she had never seen (Twain 133), she might be a "sorceress".

Another issue raised was the two rings she wore. The rings were engraved with images of Jesus and Mary, and she was asked if she had ever cured a sick person by simply touching him with the rings (Twain 352). Questions were also asked about miracles, especially those that brought dead children back to life, and suspicions were raised that they were not miracles but witchcraft (J.A. 362).

It was also pointed out that when she was imprisoned at Beaurevoir, the act of trying to escape by jumping off the roof may have constituted suicide, a forbidden act in Christianity (J.A. 362).

As stated in the 12 Articles of Accusation, Joan refused to obey the Church, threatened those who disobeyed her, testified that everything she did was by divine command, that she had never committed any sin, that she dressed as a man, which was forbidden, and that she said that St. Catherine and St. Marguerite was on the French side, which was the reason he was labeled a heretic (J.A. 385).

The narrator, Conte, however, criticizes these statements as completely untrue. According to Conte, Joan described all her acts to Rouen's court and has not disobeyed the church (J.A. 385). He also asserts that she made no threats against those who would not obey her.

And only her feats, Conte sees, were carried out by divine decree, the other things she did of her own volition (J.A. 385). He also cites that he had received permission from the Catholic Archbishop of Reims and the Tribunal of Poitiers for wearing men's clothes (J.A. 385). Conte also adds that Joan did not know the Bible (J.A. 387).

Clearly, Twain's portrayal of Joan was intended to draw a contradiction between the Christians' preaching of the importance of neighborly love and the cruelty of the burnings they carried out. A quote expresses Twain's anger at God for having tacitly approved the punishment of burning at the stake for the pious and faithful Joan of Arc.

> Then the pitchy smoke, shot through with red flashes of flame, rolled up in a thick volume and hid her from sight; and from the heart of this darkness her voice rose strong and eloquent in prayer, and when by moments the wind shredded somewhat of the smoke aside, there were veiled glimpses of an upturned face and moving lips. At last a mercifully swift tide of flame burst upward, and none saw that face any more nor that form, and the voice was still.

> Yes, she was gone from us: JOAN OF ARC! What little words they are, to tell of a rich world made empty and poor! (*J.A.* 440)

It is striking at this point when Joan tells the hypocritical priest, "Bishop, it is by you that I die!" (*J.A.* 434). By nature, a priest is a servant of God. The sentence that the bishop handed down was the death penalty.

In the above quote, the most foolish and hypocritical acts of mankind have turned young Joan's vibrant world into a gray one. Twain's description of the angelic girl's final days expresses his anger at God, as he concludes that the "rich world" has become an empty, poor world. The fact that Joan did not voluntarily go to war, but rather followed God's mandate, led to Twain's criticism of God.

There are places where Joan was the happiest when she was at Domrémy.

> I was not ever fond of wounds and suffering, nor fitted by my nature to inflict them; and quarrellings did always distress me, and noise and tumult were against my liking, my disposition being toward peace and quietness, and love for all things that have life; and being made like this, how could I bear to think of wars and blood, and the pain that goes with them, and the sorrow and mourning that follow after? But by his angels God laid His great commands upon me, and could I disobey? I did as I was bid. Did He command me to do many things?

No; only two: to raise the siege of Orléans, and crown the King at Rheims. The task is finished, and I am free. Has ever a poor soldier fallen in my sight, whether friend or foe, and I not felt the pain in my own body, and the grief of his home-mates in my own heart? No, not one; and, oh, it is such bliss to know that my release is won, and that I shall not any more see these cruel things or suffer these tortures of the mind again! Then why should I not go to my village and be as I was before? It is heaven! and ye wonder that I desire it. Ah, ye are men — just men! My mother would understand. (*J.A.* 275)

It is clear from the above quote that Joan did not like being a commander. Conflict and bloodshed did not suit her nature at all. Twain's Joan is a natural man character who enjoys her freedom in the woods of the village of Domrémy, where she is friends with animals and fairies. Domrémy was a place of relaxation for Joan, but God's voice sent her to the battlefield. Although she had accomplished two great feats, the liberation of Orleans and the coronation in Reims, she was appointed commander-in-chief again, this time at the request of her country. Then, having fought and led France to victory, she is treated like a witch after her capture at Compiègne. Twain's Joan, a 19-year-old innocent woman of nature, sacrificed her youth to protect the French people, but her loyalty is perverted and she is stigmatized as a heretic. In the end, her own people stood by and King Charles VII did nothing to prevent Joan's execution in Rouen. Her last request for water went unheeded. Twain strongly denounces in this story the hypocrisy and stupidity of God and the people who remained silent over the death of innocent Joan.

What was Joan's message? It was that life in a normal, peaceful village is the happiest life, and going to war is mentally and physically constraining and deprives people of their freedom. The message of the work itself is an indictment of God's sin in sending Joan, a healthy, innocent girl in the midst of her youth, to the battlefield and of the folly and betrayal of her countrymen. Twain emphasizes the tragic consequences of turning the presence of the natural man, Joan of Arc, from an angel to a demon.

Section 3: *The Chronicle of Young Satan* (1969); What is God to Satan?

In *The Chronicle of Young Satan*, there is no direct blasphemous scene, but an old woman named Ursula finds a stray cat, takes pity on it, and says that God will surely help it, but Satan asks her how she could possibly know that.

> Ursula bridled at this, and said— "Perhaps you would like to have it. You must be rich, with your fine clothes and quality airs." Then she sniffed, and said, "Give it to the rich—the idea! The rich don't care for anybody but themselves; it's only the poor that have feeling for the poor, and help them. The poor and God. God will provide for this kitten."
>
> [Young Satan]: "What makes you think so?"
>
> Ursula's eyes snapped with anger.
>
> [Ursula]: "Because I know it!" she said. "Not a sparrow falls to the ground without His seeing it."
>
> [Young Satan]: "But it falls, just the same. What good is seeing it fall?"
>
> Old Ursula's jaws worked, but she could not get any words out for a moment, she was so horrified. *(C.Y.S., The Mysterious Stranger Manuscripts* 65)

This is the moment when God's stereotype as a helper and friend of the weak is shattered. This is another moment when Twain's skepticism toward God is conveyed.

We have already mentioned that Satan, who is also the main character, criticizes civilization in Chapter 8 of Part I, "The Relevance of Twain and Natural Man". The actual quote is given below.

> You must never picture Satan as a solitary, but always with a lot of vagrant animals tagging around after him. Animals could not let him alone, they were so fascinated with him; and this was mutual, for he felt the same way toward them. […] they were fond of each other because in a manner they were kin, through their mutual property in the absence of the Moral sense. And kin in another particular,

too—to him, as to them, there were no unpleasant smells. He said that unpleasant smells were an invention of Civilization—like modesty, and indecency. [...] He said that the natural man, savage, had no prejudices about smells, and no shame for his God-made nakedness. (*C.Y.S.*, *The Mysterious Stranger Manuscript* 139)

It is interesting that natural man and Satan have something in common. Betty F Rainey has analyzed this passage from a different perspective than the author.

This young sceptic always remembered his mother's pity for Satan as the most lost of all the wicked, and he began to feel akin to this lost being. [...] *The Mysterious Stranger* depicts the young Sam and Satan as one, residing in Hannibal and being appreciated by the animals, since they too were lacking the Moral Sense. [...] There is evidence that at this time Sam believed in predestination, because he seemed to view himself as one of the doomed. He considered becoming a minister, since it seemed the only possible road to salvation for him. But he later learned that this was not security either. At eighteen, Sam was still a "silent rebel"; he questioned the existence of God, hell, Satan, and heaven. Whether or not he ever answered the questions concerning these topics, he would find an outlet for discussing them in fiction and nonfiction until his death. (Rainey 19)

Section 4: *Letters from the Earth* (1962)

The boy Satan in *The Chronicle of Young Satan* says that his uncle is Satan (Lucifer) and that he was banished from God. Satan, who is also thought to be Lucifer in *Letters from the Earth*, is also banished and this adult Satan is a more extensive critic of God. It is one of Twain's most bitter criticisms of God's actions as experimental, written in his later years. It is a well-known perception of Christian values that God is absolute, perfect, and sublime, but Twain's incomprehension, disbelief, and anger toward God were probably compounded by the deaths of his relatives that occurred one after the other.

Twain may have maintained his Christian faith, as mentioned above, but his criticism of God in his later works clearly shows his strong doubt about God at that time. Both *Letters from the Earth* and *The Chronicle of Young Satan* are negative about God's actions. For instance, this scene in which Satan asks God why he created the animals, and God answers him.

"Divine One," said Satan, making obeisance, "what are they for?"

"They are an experiment in Morals and Conduct. Observe them and be instructed." (*L.F.E.* 5)[20]

In other words, God considers animal experimentation a "new method of morality and action." The fact that animals are not only created but also used as tools for experimentation suggests that Twain's view of God is filled with skepticism.

This quote is from Satan, who questions the justification for animals killing and eating other animals to live.

There were thousands of them [animals]. They were full of activities. Busy, all busy—mainly in persecuting each other. Satan remarked—after examining one of them through a powerful microscope: "This large beast is killing weaker animals, Divine One."

"The tiger—yes. The law of his nature is ferocity. The law of his nature is the Law of God. He cannot disobey it."

"Then in obeying it he commits no offense, Divine One?"

"No, he is blameless."

"This other creature, here, is timid, Divine One, and suffers death without resisting."

"The rabbit—yes. He is without courage. It is the law of his nature— the Law of God. He must obey it."

"Then he cannot honorably be required to go counter to his nature and resist, Divine One?"

"No. No creature can be honorably required to go counter to the law of his nature— the Law of God."

---

[20] Abbreviation for *Letters from the Earth.*

After a long time and many questions, Satan said, "The spider kills the fly, and eats it; the bird kills the spider and eats it; the wildcat kills the goose; the—well, they all kill each other. It is murder all along the line. Here are countless multitudes of creatures, and they all kill, kill, kill, they are all murderers. And they are not to blame, Divine One? " (*LFE* 5-6)

What is important about this scene is that God has decreed the laws of nature. In other words, it is God who authorizes all the killing that occurs. The description of human beings as nothing more than the "noblest work of God" (7) can also be taken as a criticism of God's treatment of human beings as objects.

The following quotation, which asserts that God does not listen to human prayers, also reveals God's irony.

He [man] prays for help, and favor, and protection, every day; and does it with hopefulness and confidence, too, although no prayer of his has ever been answered. The daily affront, the daily defeat, do not discourage him, he goes on praying just the same. There is something almost fine about this perseverance. I must put one more strain upon you: he thinks he is going to heaven! (*L.F.E.* 8)

Satan, after sarcastically commenting on these human loyalty to God, also complains bitterly about God's creation of Adam and Eve.

He made a man and a woman and placed them in a pleasant garden, along with the other creatures. They all lived together there in harmony and contentment and blooming youth for some time; then trouble came. God had warned the man and the woman that they must not eat of the fruit of a certain tree. And he added a most strange remark: he said that if they ate of it they should surely die. Strange, for the reason that inasmuch as they had never seen a sample death they could not possibly know what he meant. Neither would he nor any other god have been able to make those ignorant children understand what was meant, without furnishing a sample. The mere word could have no meaning for them, any more than it would have for an infant of days. (*L.F.E.*16-17)

In other words, Satan claims that Adam and Eve are not to blame for eating the forbidden fruit, but that God is to blame for giving them contradictory choices in their ignorance. Then, the serpent comes and seduces them, telling them that they will gain wisdom if they eat the fruit of the forbidden tree.

> Presently a serpent sought them out privately, and came to them walking upright, which was the way of serpents in those days. The serpent said the forbidden fruit would store their vacant minds with knowledge. So they ate it, which was quite natural, for man is so made that he eagerly wants to know. (*L.F.E.*17)

Twain is sympathetic toward Adam and Eve and critical of God.

> He elected to punish *their* children, all through the ages to the end of time, for a trifling offense committed by others before they were born. (*L.F.E.*20)

Satan is criticizing the absurdity of imputing eternal guilt on the two and their descendants for an inconsequential sin. Furthermore, Satan argues that God is the creator of hell:

> In time, the Deity perceived that death was a mistake; a mistake, in that it was insufficient; insufficient, for the reason that while it was an admirable agent for the inflicting of misery upon the survivor, it allowed the dead person himself to escape from all further persecution in the blessed refuge of the grave. This was not satisfactory. A way must be conceived to pursue the dead beyond the tomb.

> The Deity pondered this matter during four thousand years unsuccessfully, but as soon as he came down to earth and became a Christian his mind cleared and he knew what to do. He invented hell, and proclaimed it. (*L.F.E.*45)

In other words, God devised hell to make humans suffer even more after death. The emphasis here is on God's cruelty.

As we have seen, we can infer a message of criticism of God by the natural man character in the works Twain wrote in his later years. However, the message of the natural man character is not directed only against God.

It also discusses the social conditions surrounding Huck at that time, the feudal system of the time in which Joan was living, and the problematic nature of people's attitudes and values.

CHAPTER 3

TWAIN AND RELIGION

Section 1: Twain and Freemasonry

As previously mentioned, Twain's religious views are complex and inconsistent. From an early age, Twain attended church and continued to do so in his later years.

Although Twain attended church as a child, he became a member of the Freemasons[21] in 1861 (Uenishi 13). He did not leave Freemasonry until 1869 (Twain, *Autobiography of Mark Twain. Volume 3*. 637). The following is a summary of the organization of Freemasonry:

> The Freemasons are a fraternal organization that emerged between 16th and 17th centuries in Europe and has since spread globally, becoming one of the largest in the world, with over 5 million worldwide members and over 2 million in the United States alone. Over the centuries, the Freemasons have attracted a host of powerful members from the politically and socially elite communities. The elite membership of the group, coupled with unusual and secretive

---

[21]   Quotation from "Freemasonry" by Hiroshi Aramata (1)

Much of the knowledge explored by Freemasons involved fields that could be called natural sciences because they believed in grasping the truth through rational logic. At the same time, however, there was also a Faustian passion for the wisdom of antiquity, that is, the way of knowledge that tries to take up as much of the old wisdom as possible. These two things brought together people who were not satisfied with the Christian teachings that existed at the time. It was a movement in a different direction from the old but equally great search for truth. Freemasonry played what might be called the guardian role in that quest (266).

rituals and symbolism, has made the Freemason a popular subject for the various conspiracy theories. According to the group's own description, the Freemason host gatherings of like-minded individuals for the express purpose of spiritual and intellectual enlightenment. Critics of the organization have accused the Freemasons of a variety of more sinister and secretive activities, from supporting military factions like the Nazis, and White Power organizations, like the Ku Klux Klan, to actively recruiting influential individuals and raising funds to forward a goal of global Freemasons are a satanic cult and a holdover from an ancient struggle between dark faiths in opposition to Christianity. (Issitt 53)

The date of the founding of Freemasonry is June 24, 1717 (Aramata 25), and Freemasonry is said to have two sources.

The first stream originated in the Mason's professional associations, which have been clearly documented since the Middle Ages. Today's Freemasonry members call this the "Practical Mason" stream. This is the history of craftsmen who had geometric knowledge, could cut stone, and could undertake building projects. The second stream, on the other hand, is the history of enlightened (illuminated) people who have been crying out for "the betterment of the world" by enlightened people who have awakened to knowledge. Those who belong to this stream are now called "speculative" Masons. They are not masons, but a group of cultured people who understood mathematics and geometry and tried to improve the world system with rational ideas. (Aramata 24-25, cited and translated by Taro Maeyashiki)

There is no doubt that membership in Freemasonry would have broadened Twain's worldview and religious views. James Wilson shows Twain's attitude toward Rationalism as follows: "Twain's attitude toward Rationalism was that of a man who was a member of the Freemasons." What other religious views besides Freemasonry might have influenced Twain's view of thought? Twain met Joseph Twichell, the pastor of a Congregationalist church in Asylum Hill, during a visit to Hartford, and they remained friends for the next 40 years.

Samuel Clemens found the religious climate at Twichell's church congenial with the comfortable deism into which he had settled in the decade after his 1870 marriage to Olivia. (Wilson, LeMaster ed. *The Mark Twain Encyclopedia* 757)

The following is an account by Roberta S. Trites of the Twitchell Church's influence on Twain's spiritualism:

> Samuel Clemens attended Joseph Twichell's Asylum Hill Congregational Church in Hartford. While Clemens never formally joined the church, he did rent a pew for his family and regularly went to church there. More important, he had an intimate friendship with Twichell that influenced Clemens's spirituality throughout his adult life. (Trites 55)

Twain's wife Olivia trusted Twitchell. Twitchell was also present at the funerals of all of Twain's family members: his oldest daughters Susy and Olivia and his third daughter Jean (Kamei 293).

Section 2: Twain's Autobiography and Satan

As Asahi has already mentioned, his autobiography shows that Twain had special feelings for Satan.

> And I have always felt friendly toward Satan. Of course that is ancestral; it must be in the blood, for I could not have originated it. (Twain, *Autobiography of Mark Twain. Volume 1*, 204)

What is interesting here is that he attributes such feelings toward Satan to the blood of his ancestors. Twain's interest in Freemasonry, with its connection to the gods of the underworld[22], is probably another reason for his rich view of Satan.

---

[22] Quotes from "Freemasonry" by Hiroshi Aramata (2)

The most famous of the mysteries performed in Egypt is the Mysterion of Isis. The Secret Rite of Isis is presided over by a mountain dog-headed god named Anubis. Anubis is the ancient Egyptian god of mummies. In other words, he is a god who deals with the dead. What was the content of this secret ceremony of Isis? Osiris, the husband of Isis and the god of wisdom, was killed and his corpse was dismembered, after which all the bodies were recovered, returned to one body, and resurrected. One of the tenets of Freemasonry is that "the fragmented Wisdom into one," which is exactly what Isis's legend alludes to (Aramata 232-233, cited and translated by Taro Maeyashiki).

Section 3: Twain's Later Years and Works

Several of Twain's later works imply disillusionment with Christianity and criticism of God. One of the first reasons for this may be the deaths of his relatives that occurred one after another: in 1890, his mother, Jane, died at the age of 87; in 1896, his eldest daughter, Susy, died of encephalitis at the age of 24; in 1897, his brother Orion died; in 1904, his wife Olivia, aged 58, died in Florence; and in 1909 both his sister Pamela died and his third daughter Jean, suddenly, at the age of 29. Thus, Twain's later years were bleak, with a succession of relatives' deaths. These realities surely increased Twain's doubts about God. Moreover, Twain condemns the state of the world from the perspective of the natural man character.

Section 4: Changes in Twain's Religious Views

According to Tetsuo Uenishi's "Religious Frontiers," Twain's original religious views were Christian. He attended a Presbyterian church with his mother (Uenishi 13). However, Twain was not exclusively influenced by Christianity during his childhood. Twain's mother sometimes resorted to medical practices based on folk beliefs. It is also possible that Twain was influenced by mysticism, as a mesmerist visited Hannibal (Uenishi 14). Twain also had contact with an African American slave owned by his uncle who believed in voodoo (Uenishi 13-14). Voodoo includes ancestor worship and is related to nature worship. Jim, the African American man *in Adventures of Huckleberry Finn,* also believed in voodoo and used a cow's hairball to tell fortunes. In 1861, Twain joined the Freemasons and is said to have developed Enlightenment-style rationalist thought (Uenishi 15). Twain continued to attend Presbyterian churches in Nevada in 1862 and in San Francisco from 1865, where he became friends with the pastors (Uenishi 13).

Various other studies have been conducted on Twain's religious transition. Shizuyo Masui discusses Twain's religious views in her article "Mark Twain and the Age of Evangelicalism." Masui cites Cummings' description of Twain's religious transition in Sherwood P. Cummings' *Mark Twain and Science* (1988). The following were quoted and translated by Masui from Cummings when writing the paper:

(1) "Calvinism": Hannibal's boyhood until about age 17.

(2) "Evangelical Christianity" 1868-1870, a period of interaction with East Coast Protestantism through his meeting with Olivia, who would become his wife

(3) "Post-Darwinist scientism," 1871, the period of influence of evolutionary theory.

(4) "Theism" 1891, an era inclined toward theism

(*Journal of Mark Twain Studies*, Issue number 8, 43)

Shizuyo Masui also notes that "Twain maintained the Calvinistic doctrine of the fall of human nature throughout his life" (52). Although Twain was critical of Christianity, he apparently tried to remain a Christian.

Harold K. Bush gives the following description of his father, John Marshall Clemens (August 11, 1798–March 24, 1847), who influenced Twain's thinking:

> [...] Sam's father is probably best typified as a freethinker, a category of religious sensibility sharply on the rise in the nineteenth century with roots in Enlightenment deism and manifested most publicly in the Masonic movement of which John was a member. Mark Twain would follow his father into both of these avocations in later years, to varying degrees. (Bush 31)

It is certain that Twain's father's influence was the basis for his membership in Freemasonry. Mr. Bush further describes "freethought":

> Although freethinking or "freethought" is generally considered to be the equivalent of agnosticism or even atheism, in its antebellum forms it need not have been so understood. Rather, freethought was "a phenomenon running the gamut from the truly antireligious—to those who regarded all religion as a form of superstition and wished to reduce its influence in every aspect of society—to those who adhered to a private, unconventional faith revering some form of God or Providence but at odds with orthodox religious authority. (Bush 31)

This range of ideas from true atheism to non- or anti-religious faith contributed to the complexity of Twain's view of Christianity.

Along this spectrum of freethinking, the former version emphasizing antireligious zeal would generally come after the onslaught of the Civil War, evolutionary science, biblical criticism, and the influence of the preeminent "free-thinker" of the century, Col. Robert G. Ingersoll, whom Mark Twain greatly admired later in his life. John Clemens would have been closer to the earlier, deist version of freethinking—asserting the reality of God but questioning the authority of earthly institutions claiming to speak for that God. Such a milder form of freethought made its most obvious American appearance in the writings of Thomas Paine, especially *The Age of Reason*, a book that Twain swallowed whole and nearly memorized in about 1857.

[…]

It is conceivable that Twain heard most of Thomas Paine's ideas from his father and uncle in his youth, but Twain later claimed to have read Paine only when he was a cub pilot. He remembered reading *The Age of Reason* "with fear and hesitation, but marveling at its fearlessness and wonderful power." Arguably it was of all books the one most definitive in the forming the philosophy of the mature Mark Twain, although perhaps in an unconscious way that remains hard to document. (Bush 31-32)

Section 5: Twain's Lecture (Religion)

As Rainey has already mentioned, Twain also had aspirations to become a pastor around the time he decided to become a writer in the West. However, Twain sometimes expressed contradictory opinions on the existence of the Christian God at the same time, indicating that his belief in God was wavering. Some of his statements are close to atheism, depending on your point of view, and will be discussed from the following example.

Twain spoke at Tuskegee, a teachers' college founded by Booker T. Washington in 1881, in January 1906 as the co-chair of an event to raise funds for what is now Tuskegee University. The following is from his speech.

> There being nothing to explain, nothing to refute, nothing to excuse, there is nothing left for me to do now but resume my nature trade—which is teaching. At Tuskegee they thoroughly ground the student in the Christian code of morals; they instill into him the indisputable truth that this is the highest and best of all systems of morals; that the Nation's greatness, its strength, and its repute among the other nation is the product of that system; that it is the foundation upon which rests the American character; that whatever is commendable, whatever is valuable in the individual American's character is the flower of fruit of that seed.
>
> They teach him that this is true in every case, whether the man be a professing Christian or an unbeliever; for we have none but the Christian code of morals, and every individual is under its character-building powerful influence and dominion from the cradle to the grave; he breathes it in with his breath, it is in his blood and bone, it is the web and woof and fibre of his mental and spiritual heredities and ineradicable. And so every born American among the eighty millions, let his creed or destitution of creed be what it may, is indisputably a Christian to this degree—that his moral constitution is Christian. (Twain, *Autobiography of Mark Twain. Volume 1.* 306)

Certainly, as a Christian society, most American people are under the influence of Christianity as they are baptized from birth and continue to attend church. Christianity is culturally ingrained in the United States, unlike in Japan, and has considerable influence. So what then did Twain say about the Christian moral code?

> All this is true, and no student will leave Tuskegee ignorant of it. Then what will he lack under his head? What is there for me to teach him under this head that he may possibly not acquire there, or may acquire in a not sufficiently emphasized form? Why this large fact, this important fact—that there are two separate and district kinds of Christian morals, so separate, so distinct, so unrelated that they are

no more kin to each other than are archangels and politicians. The one kind is Christian private morals, the other is Christian public morals. (*Autobiography of Mark Twain, vol.1* 306)

This passage is important because it is the first of these two kinds of morals that is most important. In *Adventures of Huckleberry Finn*, Huck puts his personal moral code first and resists the public moral code, thus ignoring the slave laws set forth by the government of what was then a Christian society, the United States, to help Jim. The question Twain is posing here is which is more important: public moral law or individual moral law?

> The loyal observance of Christian private morals has made this Nation what it is—a clean and upright people in its private domestic life, an honest and honorable people in its private commercial life; no alien nation can claim superiority over it in these regards, no critic foreign domestic, can challenge the validity of this truth. During 363 days in the year the American citizen is true to his Christian private morals, and keeps undefiled the Nation's character at its best and highest; then in the other two days of the year he leaves his Christian private morals at home, and carries his Christian public morals to the tax office and the polls and does the best he can to damage and undo his whole year's faithful and righteous worth. (*Autobiography of Mark Twain, vol.1*, 306)

From the speech so far, it is possible to interpret Twain's emphasis on Christian values. The content of the speech can be understood to be about how the Christian moral code contributed to shape the character of each individual citizen and building the nation. Reading this passage alone would have led one to conclude that Twain's religious views were still rooted in Christianity. It is true that Twain's beloved wife, Olivia, was a devout Christian, and Twain was accepted into the Langdon family because he shared her beliefs. It was a condition of their marriage that they would adhere to their beliefs as Christians. Agreement on religious beliefs between husband and wife is important in American society. In fact, Twain's feelings and opinions about Christianity are evident in his works.

However, Twain also gave a speech in June of the same year, in which he stated the exact opposite of his views on God. It is hard to believe that this is the same Twain who gave the speech.

Let us now consider the real God, the genuine God, the great God, the sublime and supreme God, the authentic Creator of the *real* universe, whose remoteness are visited by comets only—comets unto which incredibly distant Neptune is merely an outpost, a Sandy Hook to homeward bound spectres of the deeps of space that have not glimpsed it before for generations—a universe not made with hands and suited to an astronomical nursery, but spread abroad through the illimitable grandeur and majesty, by comparison with whom all the other gods whose myriads infest the feeble imaginations of men are as a swarm of gnats scattered and lost in the infinitudes of the empty sky. (*Autobiography of Mark Twain, vol. 2* 136)

When Twain begins his discussion of "the real God," he lists the adjectives for "God" as "the real God, the genuine God, the great God." The number of adjectives undermines the value of the noun being described. It is a form of sarcasm and irony and leads to a negative evaluation of God, indicating an antipathy toward the sublime being God. God is too far away and can only be visited by comets. Neptune is simply an outpost. The universe is not made by hand but extends infinitely. Compared to this sublime "God," the poor imaginary gods of people are no better than a swarm of gnats in an infinite void.

When we think of such a God as this, we cannot associate with him anything trivial, anything lacking dignity, anything lacking grandeur. We cannot conceive of His passing by Sirius to choose our potato for a footstool. We cannot conceive of His interesting Himself in the affairs of the microscopic human race and enjoying its Sunday flatteries, and experiencing pangs of jealousy when flatteries grow lax or fail, any more than we can conceive of the Emperor of China being interested in a bottle of microbes and pathetically anxious to stand well with them and harvest their impertinent compliments. If we could conceive of the Emperor of China taking an intemperate interest in his bottle of microbes, we should have to draw the line there; we could not, by any stretch of imagination, conceive of his selecting from these innumerable millions a quarter of a thimbleful of Jew microbes—the least attractive of the whole swarm—and making pets of them and nominating them as his chosen germs, and carrying his infatuation for them so far as to resolve to keep and coddle them alone, and damn all the rest. (*Autobiography of Mark Twain, vol.2*, 136)

According to Twain, it is inconceivable that in thinking about the "true God" in this way, such a god would favor one tiny quantity of insignificant beings over another – that he would consider Christians as being correct and true over all the rest. Humans couldn't possibly matter enough.

When we examine the myriad wonders and glories and charms and perfections of this infinite universe(as we know the universe now), and perceive that there is not a detail of it—from the blade of grass to the giant trees of California, not from the obscure mountain rivulet to the measureless ocean; nor from the ebb and flow of the tides to the stately motions of the planets—that is not the slave of a system of exact and inflexible law, we seem to know—not suppose nor conjecture, but *know*—that the God that brought this stupendous fabric into being with a flash of thought and framed its laws with another flash of thought, is endowed with limitless power. [...] We seem to know that when He flashed the universe into being He foresaw everything that would happen in it from that moment until the end of time. (*Autobiography of Mark Twain, vol.2*, 137)

Here Twain points out that if we look at the universe as understood at the time, we know everything in it is governed by an array of immutable laws of physics. In which case, if it was all created by God, he would therefore immediately know everything that would happen within that system to its end. In short, Twain is continuing to convey the message that if you observe people from a cosmic perspective, the prejudices people have are extremely trivial and it is foolish to dwell on them.

Do we also know that He is a moral being, according to our standard of morals? No. If we know anything at all about it, we know that He is destitute of morals—at least of the human pattern. Do we know that He is just, charitable, kindly, gentle, merciful, compassionate? No. There is no evidence that he is any of these things,—whereas each and every day, as it passes, furnishes us a thousand volumes of evidence, and indeed proof, that he possesses none of these qualities. (*Autobiography of Mark Twain, vol.2*, 137)

Here, Twain states that God lacks morality, that is, he lacks reason, the opposite of what he said in the speech we discussed before. This speech is more likely to be Twain's real intention than the previous one. The content of this speech is closer to that of Twain's works and thoughts in his later years. Even Tom and Huck are God-fearing but also skeptical of Christianity; Huck is out of step with the Christian discipline of the time because he aided and abetted slaves in violation of public morality. However, it is a fact that Twain was close to his beloved wife Olivia's Christian faith, so it is impossible to identify his religious views in general. To what extent did Twain's doubts about God deepen?

When we pray, when we beg, when we implore, does He listen? Does He answer? There is not a single authentic instance of it in human history. Does He silently refuse to listen—refuse to answer? There is nothing resembling to proof that He has ever done anything else. From the beginning of time, priests, who have imagined themselves to be His appointed and salaried servants, have gathered together their full numerical strength and simultaneously prayed for rain, and never once got it, when it was not due according to the eternal laws of Nature. Whenever they got it, if they had had a competent Weather Bureau they could have told them it was coming, anyhow, within twenty-four hours, whether they prayed or saved their sacred wind. (*Autobiography of Mark Twain, vol.2*, 137)

When we pray, when we plead, does God hear us, Twain asks his audience? He posits that no such thing has ever happened in the history of man. With a competent weather forecast to say whether or not rain would fall within 24 hours, there would be no need for priests and their congregations to pray for rain. In other words, Twain emphasizes the pointlessness of praying.

This speech was made in 1906, by which time Twain had lost several family members. Twain's attitude toward the deaths of his relatives would have been to "pray" even if he had not been a Christian. However, his act of praying was in vain, and one after another, Twain suffered their disastrous deaths. Through this process, Twain may have learned the transience of life, and at the same time, he may have felt the meaninglessness and futility of praying at the same time.

> From the beginning of time, whenever a king has lain dangerously ill, the priesthood and some part of the nation have prayed in unison that the kind be spared to his grieving and anxious people(in case they were grieving and anxious, which was not usually the rule)and in no instance was their prayer ever answered. When Mr. Garfield lay near to death, the physicians and surgeons knew that nothing could save him, yet at an appointed signal all the pulpits in the United States broke forth with one simultaneous and supplicating appeal for the President's restoration to health. They did this with the same old innocent confidence with which the primeval savage had prayed to his imaginary devils to spare his perishing chief—for that day will never come when facts and experience can teach a pulpit anything useful. Of course the President died, just the same. (*Autobiography of Mark Twain vol.2*, 137)

It is conceivable that Twain's skepticism about God as a savior would have spilled over into every thought. Had he lived the rest of his life happily without suffering the death of a relative, he would not have been so pessimistic. Twain's thoughts would have expanded from the death of his relatives to the world at large, and his pessimism would have deepened as his attention shifted to the futility of this world. There is more to this speech. Was Twain's opinion on the efficacy of prayer consistent?

> Great Britain has a population of forty-one millions. She has eighty thousand pulpits. The Boer population was a hundred and fifty thousand, with a battery of two hundred and ten pulpits. In the beginning of the Boer war, at a signal from the Primate of all England, the eighty thousand English pulpits thundered forth a titanic simultaneous supplication to their God to give the embattled

English in South Africa the victory. The little Boer battery of two hundred and ten guns replied with a simultaneous supplication for the same God to give the Boers the victory. If the eighty thousand English clergy had left their prayers unshed and gone to the field, they would have got it—whereas the victory went the other way, and the English forces suffered defeat after defeat at the hands of the Boers. The English pulpit kept discreetly quiet about the result of its effort, but the indiscreet Boer pulpit proclaimed with a loud and exultant voice that it was *its* prayers that had conferred the victory upon the Boers. (*Autobiography of Mark Twain vol.2*, 137-138)

In essence, Twain is advocating a kind of God-critical view in which the act of prayer is declared to have effects on reality that have nothing to do with it.

The British Government had more confidence in soldiers than in prayer—therefore instead of doubling and trebling the numerical strength of the clergy it doubled and trebled the strength of its forces in the field. Then the thing happened that always happens— the English whipped the fight, a rather a plain indication that the Lord had not listened to either side, and was as indifferent as to who should win as He had always been, from the day that He was evolved, down to the present time—there being no instance on record where He has shown any interest at all in any human squabble, nor whether the good cause won out or lost. (*Autobiography of Mark Twain vol.2*, 138)

Twain emphasizes that God has been indifferent to human conflicts from the beginning until now. Whether the reason for the fight was good or bad, Twain explains, was not a matter of curiosity to God.

Has this experience taught the pulpit anything? It has not. When the Boer prayers achieved victory—as the Boers believed—the Boers were confirmed once more in their trust in the power of prayer. When a crushing finality of defeat overwhelmed them, later, in the face of their confident supplications, their attitude was not altered, nor their confidence in the righteousness and intelligence of God impaired. (*Autobiography of Mark Twain vol.2* 138)

Did these experiences teach the clergy anything, Twain asks? They taught them nothing. When Boer prayers led to victory, and when they were later defeated, they did not lose their trust in God regardless. The speech could be seen as ironic and sympathetic to the Boers, who continued to pray even when their prayers to God were not heard.

> Often we see a mother who has been despoiled, little by little, of everything she held dear in life but a sole remaining dying child; we have seen her, I say, kneeling by its bed and pouring out from a breaking heart beseechings to God for mercy that would get glad and instant answer from any man who had the power to save that child— yet no such prayer has ever moved a God to pity. Has that mother been convinced? Sometimes—but only for a little while. She was merely a human being, and the like the rest—ready to pray again in the next emergency; ready to believe again that she would be heard. (*Autobiography of Mark Twain vol.2* 138)

Twain may have had a hard time understanding his mother's attitude of continuing to pray even when her wishes were not granted, and falling back on prayer even after losing her child, but he must have been moved by such a situation.

> We know that the real God, the Supreme God, the actual Maker of the universe, made everything that is in it. We know that He made all the creatures, from the microbe and the brontosaur down to man and the monkey, and that he knew what would happen to each and every one of them, from the beginning of time to the end of it. In the case of each, creature, big or little, He made it an unchanging law that that creature should suffer wanton and unnecessary pains and miseries every day of its life—that by that law these pains and miseries could not be avoided by any diplomacy exercisable by the creature; that its way, from birth to death, should be beset by traps, pitfalls, and gins, ingeniously planned and ingeniously concealed; and that by another law every transgression of a law of Nature,

either ignorantly or wittingly committed, should in every instance be visited by a punishment ten-thousandfold out of proportion to the transgression. (*Autobiography of Mark Twain vol.2* 138)

Returning to the unfeeling, all-foreseeing creator God, Twain explains that his inexorable natural laws condemn all life to misery, and the punishment for breaching those natural laws is always ridiculously disproportionate. According to Twin, if life is full of pain and cruelty, it is because God has set it up in such a way.

> We stand astonished at the all-comprehensive malice which could patiently descend to the contriving of elaborate tortures for the meanest and pitifulest of the countless kinds of creatures that were to inhabit the earth. The spider was so contrived that she would not eat grass, but must catch flies, and such things, and inflict a slow and horrible death upon them, unaware that her turn would come next. The wasp was so contrived that he also would decline grass and stab the spider, not conferring upon her a swift and merciful death, but merely half paralyzing her, then ramming her down into the wasp den, there to live and suffer for days, while the wasp babies should chew her legs off at their leisure. (*Autobiography of Mark Twain vol.2* 138-139)

We would be surprised to be confronted with the fact that such malice inflicts a variety of suffering on creatures of any character, as Twain says. Living creatures kill without knowing that they are next in line.

> In turn, there was a murderer provided for the wasp, and another murderer for the wasp's murderer, and so on throughout the whole scheme of living creatures in the earth. There isn't one of them that was not designed and appointed to inflict misery and murder on some fellow creature and suffer the same, in turn, from some other murderous fellow creature. In flying into the web the fly is merely guilty of an indiscretion—not a breach of any law—yet the fly's punishment is ten-thousandfold out of proportion to that little indiscretion.

The ten-thousandfold law of punishment is rigorously enforced against every creature, man included. The debt, whether made innocently or guiltily, is promptly collected by Nature—and in this world, without waiting for the ten-billionfold additional penalty appointed—in the case of man—for collection in the next. (*Autobiography of Mark Twain vol.2* 139)

According to Twain's theory, not only is a 10,000-fold penalty is imposed on all creatures, including humans, for every unfortunate indiscretion, regardless of guilt. And unlike in Christian teaching, that punishment is enacted in this life, not the afterlife. Twain laments the misery of fate.

This system of atrocious punishment for something and nothing begins upon the helpless baby on its first day in the world, and never ceases until its last one. Is there a father who would persecute his baby with unearned colics and the unearned miseries of teething, and follow these with mumps, measles, scarlet fever, and the hundred other persecutions appointed for the unoffending creature? And then follow these, from youth to the grave, with a multitude of ten-thousandfold punishments for laws broken either by intention or indiscretion? With a fine sarcasm, we ennoble God with the title of Father—yet we know quite well that we should hang His style of father wherever we might catch him. (*Autobiography of Mark Twain vol.2* 139)

He then points out the endless unearned miseries faced by people from the moment they are born to the moment they die and asks what kind of father, as people refer to God with deep irony, would persecute their children like this. Twain's ideas about God are certainly far removed from traditional Christian thought. He is no less withering in his assessment of the clergy.

The pulpit's explanation of, and apology for, these crimes, is pathetically destitute of ingenuity. It says they are committed for the benefit of the sufferer. They are to discipline him, purify him, elevate him, train him for the society of the Deity and the angels—send him up sanctified with cancers, tumors, smallpox, and the rest of the educational plant; whereas the pulpit knows that it is stultifying itself, if it knows anything at all. It knows that if this kind of discipline is wise and salutary, we are insane not to adopt it ourselves and apply it to our children.

Does the pulpit really believe that we can improve a purifying and elevating breed of culture invented by the Almighty? It seems to me that if the pulpit honestly believed what it is preaching, in this regard, it would recommend every father to imitate the Almighty's methods. (*Autobiography of Mark Twain vol.2* 139)

Twain states that the clergy know such suffering is meaningless, and that if they honestly believed what they were preaching, they would recommend their congregation imitate God's ways and the same arbitrary cruelties on their own children.

When the pulpit has succeeded in persuading its congregation that this system has been really wisely and mercifully contrived by the Almighty to discipline and purify and elevate His children whom He so loves, the pulpit judiciously closes its mouth. It doesn't venture further, and explain why these same crimes and cruelties are inflicted upon the higher animals—the alligators, the tigers, and the rest. It even proclaims that the beasts perish—meaning that their sorrowful life begins and ends here; that they go no further; that there is no heaven for them; that neither God nor the angels, nor the redeemed, desire their society on the other side. (*Autobiography of Mark Twain vol.2*, 139-140)

Twain tells us that if a clergyman succeeds in persuading his congregation, they will be wisely silent after that. To preach means to convince them that the irrationality in this world is designed to educate and love mankind, nothing about why all other animals need to suffer too, and indeed why they are denied an afterlife afterwards. This is a statement of Twain's disillusionment.

It puts the pulpit in a comical situation, because in spite all its ingenuities of explanation and apology it convicts its God of being a wanton and pitiless tyrant in the case of the unoffending beasts. At any rate, and beyond cavil or argument, by its silence it condemns Him irrevocably as a malignant master, after having persuaded the congregation that He is constructed entirely out of compassion, righteousness, and all-pervading love. The pulpit doesn't know how to reconcile these grotesque contradictions, and it doesn't try. (*Autobiography of Mark Twain vol.2*, 140)

Here, Twain ridicules the clergy's incomprehensible position.

In His destitution of one and all of the qualities which could grace a God and invite respect for Him, and reverence, and worship, the real God, the genuine God, the Maker of the mighty universe, is just like all the other gods in the list. He proves, every day, that He takes no interest in man, nor in the other animals, further than torture them, slay them, and get weary of the eternal and changeless monotony of it. (*Autobiography of Mark Twain vol.2*, 140)

The conflicting content of the two speeches thus far indicates that Twain's views on Christianity and God are not consistent. The fact that he attended church with his mother from an early age makes it unlikely that he would have developed an attitude of outright rejection of Christianity. There was another factor that compelled him to remain true to his Christian beliefs. He had to be a Christian to marry Olivia, who was also a Christian.

She [Olivia] was a complex figure with intellectual and moral concerns that represented much of the Victorian American culture. The sentimentalized religious piety that resonates throughout the courtship letters of 1868-69 has led some critics to make the dubious assertion that Twain's "conversion" to Christianity was nothing more than a series of rhetorical moves initiated to ensure that the Langdons would endorse the courtship of their refined daughter such an outlandish, somewhat boorish roughneck from the Far West. (Bush 61)

In *The Chronicle of Young Satan*, Satan is portrayed in a positive light, emphasizing his natural man characteristics, despite his anti-Christian words and actions that are critical of God. Twain's view of Satan may have been influenced by his mother, Jane Clemens (1803-1890), who was a devout Christian but had a strange worldview sympathetic to Satan. The basis for her compassion becomes obvious when Satan's agenda comes up. While people vehemently condemned Satan, Twain's mother offered an entirely different view:

> Satan was utterly wicked and abandoned, just as these people had said; *but* would any claim that he had been treated fairly? A sinner was but a sinner; Satan was just that, like the rest. What saves the rest?—their own efforts alone? No—or none might ever be saved. To their feeble efforts is added the mighty help of pathetic, appealing, imploring prayers that go up daily out of all the churches in Christendom and out of myriads upon myriads of pitying hearts. But who prays for Satan? Who, in eighteen centuries, has had the common humanity to pray for the one sinner that needed it most, a single one, the one sinner among us all who had the highest and clearest *right* to every Christian's daily and nightly prayers, for the plain and unassailable reason that his was the first and greatest need, he being among sinners the supremest? (Twain, *The Autobiography of Mark Twain* 34)

Such an interpretation of Satan, then or today, is probably rare in the Christian community. This made a deep impression on Twain. It is quite possible to infer that this mother's view of Satan influenced Twain's view. Therefore, in addition to natural traits, Satan has unexpected characteristics such as strength, wisdom, and compassion.

The discussion thus far shows that Twain's religious views were diverse. Twain's natural man or natural man-like characters also adhered to heretical religions; even Joan of Arc was a Catholic but held animistic beliefs. The fact that it was possible to imagine characters with such mixed religious views shows that Twain himself was open and flexible in his thinking about religion. Even Twain's opinion of Satan differed from the common interpretation held by Christians.

Subsection 1: Further Consideration of Satan

As we have already seen, in addition to *The Chronicle of Young Satan*, Satan also appears in *Letters from the Earth*. Satan in *Letters from the Earth* is not the boy of *The Chronicle of Young Satan*, but is more likely to be his uncle, as mentioned earlier. This is because Satan in *Letters from the Earth* is an outspoken critic of God, thoroughly condemning God's natural laws with his own cunning logic. Satan in *The Chronicles of Young Satan* uses metaphors to slander God, but he does not overtly attack God, and we can see his humble attitude. Satan in *Letters from the Earth* is upfront about how stupid God's laws are and how humans are foolish for not realizing that, even though they are to man's great detriment. This Satan is banished to earth for saying things that insult God. In this light, the Satan in *Letters from the Earth* is the biblical Satan as Lucifer, rather than his nephew in *The Chronicles of Young Satan*, whom Twain created anew.

Subsection 2: Relevance of Native Americans and Satan

In *Huck Finn and Tom Sawyer among the Indians*, the Native Americans were heathens and as good as Satan to the white settlers. The Native Americans believed in both a good god and a bad god, and that they could benefit from the good god without praying to him, but they could not benefit from the bad god without praying to him (61). Therefore, the Native Americans honored the bad god and believed in Satan's god. Therefore, it is natural that Native Americans with such sentiments would consider themselves equal to Satan, and it is not surprising that they would be regarded as such by the whites. The brutal murder of innocent white families is seen as the work of Satan himself. However, as we have already discussed, the character Brace, a white man, considers the massacre of the Mills family by the Native Americans as Native American retaliation for the white invasion, which shows that Twain is able to see the incident from the standpoint of the Native Americans. Another possible message is that Twain will not easily judge the killing by the Native Americans, who are natural men.

In other words, what Twain is trying to say here is that Native Americans as Satan have two sides. As long as they are not attacked, they remain relatively calm and still, but if they are invaded and their sphere of life is violated, Satan's demonic feelings are aroused and they become savages. It is often said in Japan, "A god who does not touch you has no power over you." Tracing the cause of the Mills family's murder back to the beginning, the problem lay in the government's attempt to expel the Native Americans from their sphere of life at the time.

Section 3: *Letters from the Earth* and Divine Criticism

The question is why Twain allowed Satan to deliver scathing criticism of God, as seen in *Letters from the Earth,* rather than the Native Americans, who are as good as Satan. This is the author's interpretation, but perhaps Twain feared that the Native Americans might later be criticized and protested by Christians if they violated the taboo of criticizing God in the Christian world. In other words, it is possible to attack an actual person directly, but not to harm an invisible being like Satan.

Subsection 4: Natural Man and the Natural Element: Divine Criticism

We have analyzed the characteristics of natural man-like characters in several of Twain's works. The results confirm that these characters had survival skills that could only be cultivated in the wild, a desire for simplicity without greed, a desire for freedom without social restraints, animistic heretical beliefs, and a friendship with animals. It is also important to note that the natural man character explicitly conveys a message of criticism of God. Our understanding of these characters may be deepened by considering Twain's experiences as a natural man writer working in the wilds of the Mississippi River and Nevada.

Twain's change from a contemptuous view of Native Americans as "this flitting human insect" (*The Adventures of Tom Sawyer* 157) to a reverential one in his later years reflects his reevaluation of Native Americans. Twain's message was that even though the Native Americans were savages, they still cherished basic human needs such as survival skills, the desire for simplicity, and freedom.

This quote is from Twain on race:

I am quite sure (bar one) I have no race prejudices, and I think I have no color prejudices nor caste prejudices nor creed prejudices. Indeed, I know it. I can stand any society. All that I care to know is that a man is a human being—that is enough for me; he can't be any worse. (Rasmussen 57)

This certainly shows that Twain has transcended racial differences to take a broader perspective from the standpoint of being human. In *The Chronicle of Young Satan,* Twain mentions that wild beasts are far superior to humans in that they have no "moral compass." At the same time, he describes how stupid humans are. Humans are supposed to be equal, yet they wage invasions and wars as a matter of course. Twain's message through his works is how foolish these acts are in the fleeting moments of human life. He presents an opportunity to examine whether man is really superior to beasts; that is, savages, though barbaric, are far less cruel than civilized people, who have a "moral compass" and kill with impunity. In addition, regarding his critique of God, there is much that remains to be clarified about Twain's religious views. While conventional research has suggested that Twain was an atheist, recent studies have shown that his religious beliefs were shaped by his various experiences, as Uenishi and Masuda have pointed out.

Although Twain mourned the deaths of his relatives, he did not direct all of his anger toward God. It is worth noting that the public not only made the ultimate choice of aiding and abetting the recapture of a fugitive slave, but also made Huck, at the young age of 12, excessively responsible. It is also worth noting that the French, who were Joan's allies, stood by and remained silent rather than helping her after she was captured for risking her life on the battlefield. Twain's attitude toward Christian civilization from the innocent viewpoint of natural man is evident throughout his works. It can be interpreted that the natural man-like characters we have discussed so far were trying to convey the idea that we should also look at our own human defilement.

CONCLUSION

We examined the significance of Twain's natural man or natural man-like characters and their messages. In Part I, we reviewed the origins and theories of natural man and examined Twain's references to natural man in his works and interviews. Part II examines the messages of Twain's natural man-like characters. Part III discussed the message of the Native Americans, examining the evolution of Twain's view of the Native Americans. In Part IV, we discussed Satan's high regard for natural man.

Adventures of Huckleberry Finn is the story of the natural man-like characters Huck and Jim, both fugitives from the law. At the time, Jim's escape and Huck's aiding and abetting were unforgivable acts in the American South. Thus, Huck and Jim, hunted and mentally oppressed, enjoyed a brief period of mental and physical freedom on the Mississippi River, where they were beyond the reach of society's laws and regulations. As Tomlinson has already pointed out, Twain allows his characters to speak for themselves and make the case that governments that allowed slavery are morally problematic (Tomlinson 120-121).

Joan of Arc was a hero of France, but as a result, she was treated as a heretic, a witch, and died cruelly by fire at the young age of 19. She was active and victorious in the first battle to protect the French. Twain denounces God for depriving such a loving and courageous girl of her youth and freedom with the cruel measure of burning her. One of the messages that can be read from this work is the implication that Christians, as monotheists, were exclusive, as Stone says, and that the act of viewing heretical believers as enemies was foolish (Stone 87).

As Tabei highlights, Twain's view of Native Americans shifted, and this was reflected in his works (Tabei, "From White to Red"). This is probably because Twain always maintained a free mind, unencumbered by stereotypes. In *Huck Finn and Tom Sawyer Among the Indians*, the white settlers must have had much to learn from the lives of the Native Americans who lived in harmony with nature, similar to natural man, but they did not understand their traditions concerning nature, their religion rooted in animism, or their way of life, and they only pursued immediate profit. Twain's intention was to show through his characters that this was almost criminal. As Tabei and Golay (Michael lay) have noted, Twain satirized American imperialist society by introducing these anti-government views into his characters (Tabei 333-334). However, the criticism is metaphorical in nature, and can only be found by reading the work. It was probably Twain's strategy to indirectly criticize the political system of the time rather than overtly debunk it, which is more memorable to the reader.

It is important to note that in *The Chronicles of Young Satan*, Satan is a natural man character because he is critical of civilization and friendly with animals. As Hurtado highlights, Twain's reading of extra-biblical texts undoubtedly influenced his view of Satan. Moreover, as Urtado emphasizes, we now understand that the boy's act of creating a bird from clay is not a coincidence because it resembles not only the extrabiblical scriptures but also the Koran, the Islamic holy book (Hurtado 158).

It is also important to consider Twain's religious views, as he was influenced by his mother's particular view of Satan (Twain, *The Autobiography of Mark Twain* 34).

Huck, Tom, and Jim reject the moral values of the time, Joan of Arc wishes for freedom from God, and the Native Americans stress the importance of regaining the freedom and sphere of life lost through "American nationalism," as Yoshinobu Nakajima has pointed out. Through these characters, Twain manifests Coulombe's criticism of civilization (Coulombe 113) and Tomlinson's criticism of Christianity (Tomlinson 120-121). They remind us humans of the benefits of nature and conscience that we have almost forgotten. It could be interpreted as indicating that we are at a crossroads where people are becoming conscious of the stains of civilized society. The promotion of natural man characters also hints that people then and we today can prosper in harmony with nature and resistance against imperialism, which, as Tabei points out, seeks to expand territory by losing sight of nature's bounty (333-334). Through the characters in his works with naturalistic characteristics, Twain revived the view of nature that American society had lost sight of and denounced the U.S. government's path of self-indulgence. Through the tragedies of natural man characters such as Joan of Arc and Satan, Twain also denounced the contradictions and ruthlessness of a God who did not help through anguish and despair.

Twain's natural man characters acted according to their own conscience from a natural man perspective, without being influenced by the currents of the world. Twain, through the Native Americans, "natural men living in a natural state" (Rousseau, *Emile*, 369), and Huck, Jim, Joan, and others, "natural men living in a social state" (Rousseau, *Emile*, 369), sounded the alarm against those who simply accept without question received wisdom, social conventions, and established ethics and beliefs.

The Chronicle of Young Satan, his last work, is a special reflection of Twain's feelings. As Janice McIntire-Strasburg points out, he may have tried to accept the reality of the loss of his beloved wife and child by having illusions (McIntire-Strasburg 226).

Furthermore, what was confirmed in the character of the natural man in Twain's literature was the preciousness of "freedom," as Leo Marx puts it (Devanny 353): Huck, Tom, and Jim were free from the Christian norms and morality of the time; Joan of Arc held animistic religious views and distanced herself from monotheism; Satan escaped God's bondage, which created illusions and brought death to man; the Native Americans tried to gain their freedom from American nationalism.

What was freedom like for Twain, who created the natural man character that delivered such a message? He was most free when he was a pilot, proof that he himself had a natural man aspect. Twain could reflect this rare experience in his natural man characters.

WORKS CITED

Amano, Miyuki. "The Creation of Scenery." *Journal of Mark Twain Studies*, Issue No. 14. Nan'un-do, 2015.

Anderson, William. *Green Man: The Archetype of our Oneness with the Earth.* HarperCollins P, 1990.

Aramata, Hiroshi. *Freemasonry: A Mysterious Society with a Secret.* Kadokawa Shoten, 2010. (荒俣宏.「フリーメイソン―「秘密」を抱えた謎の結社」. 角川書店, 2010年.)

Arima, Yoko. "Commentary: 'Captain Stormfield's Visit to Heaven.'" *Mark Twain's Humor Masterpieces*, Sairyusha, 2015. (有馬容子.「解説：「ストームフィールド船長の天国訪問」.『マーク・トウェインユーモア傑作選』. 彩流社, 2015.)

---. "Mark Twain's Heaven." *Journal of Mark Twain Studies*, Issue No. 3. Nan'un-do, 2004. (有馬容子.「マーク・トウェインの天国」.『マーク・トウェイン研究と批評 3号』. 南雲堂, 2004年.)

Asahi, Yukiko. "Mark Twain's 'River': Reading Transfigured Nature." *Bulletin of the Faculty of Literature*, Tamagawa University, (40), 2000, 60-73. (朝日由紀子.「マーク・トウェインの「川」―変幻自在な自然を読む―」.『玉川大学文学部紀要』. (40), 2000, 60-73.)

---. "Mark Twain and Satan." *Journal of Mark Twain Studies*, Issue No. 8. Nan'un-do, 2009 .
(「マーク・トウェインとサタン」.『マーク・トウェイン研究と批評 第8号』. 南雲堂, 2009年.)

Beaumont, Ivor Mark. *Christology in Dialogue with Muslims: A Critical Analysis of Christian Presentations of Christ for Muslims from the Ninth and Twentieth Centuries.* Paternoster, 2005.

Bruce, Robert. *CliffsNotes on Twain's The Adventures of Huckleberry Finn.* Hungry Minds, Inc., 2000.

Budd, J. Louis, ed. *On Mark Twain.* Durham: Duke UP, 1987.

Bush, Harold. *Mark Twain and the Spiritual Crisis of His Age.* Tuscaloosa: The U of Alabama P,2007.

Chesbro, Daniel, James Erickson, et al. *The Gospel of Thomas: A Spiritual Interpretation for the Aquarian Age.* Findhorn P, 2012.

Coulombe, Joseph. *Mark Twain and the American West.* Columbia: U of Missouri P, 2003.

Coulter, James. *The Green Man Unmasked: A New Interpretation of An Ancient Riddle.* Bloomington: Author House, 2006.

Curran, Bob. *Walking with the Green Man: Father of the Forest, Spirit of Nature,* 2007.

Delmendo, Sharon. "Back to Bataan Once More: Pax Americana and the Pacific Theater." *Multiculturalism and Representation: Selected Essays*. ed. Reider,J. & Smith E.L, U of Hawaii P, 1996.

Dempsey, Terrell. *Searching for Jim: Slavery in Sam Clemens's World*. U of Missouri P, 2003.

Devanny, John F. "The Moral Geography of the Adventures of Huckleberry Finn". *Adventures of Huckleberry Finn: With an Introduction and Contemporary Criticism*. Ignatis P, 2009.

Ellingson, Ter. *The Myth of the Noble Savage*. U of California P, 2001.

Emerson, Everett H. *Mark Twain: A Literary Life*. U of Pennsylvania, 2000.

Foster, David. "Mark Twain on the American Character." *History of American Political Thought*. Eds. Bryan-Paul Frost and Jeffrey Sikkenga. Lexington Books, 2003.

---. "Huck Finn: Natural Man against American Convention." *History of American Political Thought*. eds. Bryan-Paul Frost and Jeffrey Sikkenga. Lexington Books, 2003.

Foster, Raymond. *Greening of the Soul*. Bridgnorth: Dreamstairway, 2009.

Fessenden, Tracy ed. *Culture and Redemption: Religion, the Secular, and American Literature*. Princeton UP, 2007.

Finkel, Michael. "The Hadza." *National Geographic Magazine* (December 2009) 94-119. Print.

Fulton, Joe B. *The Reverend Mark Twain: Theological Burlesque, Form, and Content.* The Ohio UP, 2006.

Goto, Kazuhiko. "The Man Who Loved and the Boy Who Loved Him." *Journal of Mark Twain Studies*. Issue No. 12. Nankumodo, 2013. (後藤和彦.「愛する男、愛される少年」.『マーク・トウェイン研究と批評第12号』. 南雲堂, 2013.)

Grimassi, Raven. *Spirit of the Witch: Religion & Spirituality in Contemporary Witchcraft.* Llewellyn Worldwide Ltd, 2003.

Hawke, Mykel. *Hawke's Green Beret Survival Manual.* Running P, 2009.

Hemingway, Ernest. *Green Hills of Africa*. Vintage Classics, 2004.

Hicks, Clive. *Green Man: The Archetype of Our Oneness with the Earth.* London: HarperCollins P, 1998.

Higashi, Yoshiro. "Mark Twain and Nature: An Interpretation of *The Adventures of Huckleberry Finn*." Bunkei ron Literature Series (1) , 1980, 13-34. (東義郎.「Mark Twainと自然——*The Adventures of Huckleberry Finn*の一解釈—」. (『文経論叢. 文学科篇』. (1), 1980, 13-34.)

Hone, William. *The Apocryphal New Testament*. Wildhern P, 2007.

Hurtado. W.,L. "Who read the early Christian Apocrypha?" Eds.
Andrew, Gregory, and Tuckett, Christopher. *The Oxford
Handbook of Early Christian Apocrypha*. Oxford UP, 2015.

Deguchi, Y., Kobayashi, A. and Saito, T. eds. *Encyclopedia of British
Culture in the 21st Century.* Tokyo Sho, 2009. 出口保夫, 小林章
夫, 斉藤貴子編.『21世紀イギリス文化を知る事典』. 東京書, 2009.

Egashira, Rie. "Children Who Change Their Appearance." *Journal of
Mark Twain Studies*, Issue No. 12. Nan'un-do, 2009. (江頭理江.
「姿を変える子どもたち」.『マーク・トウェイン研究と批評 第12号』. 南雲堂,
2009年.)

---. "The Meaning of the Breakaway from Mississippi." *Journal of
Mark Twain Studies*, Issue No. 5. Nan'un-do, 2009. (江頭理恵.
「ミシシッピからの離脱の意味」.『マーク・トウェイン研究と批評 第5号』. 南雲
堂, 2009年.)

Fujii, Chifuyu. "Huck's 'Nature' and 'Civilization': An Ideal Society
from the Viewpoint of 'Freedom'." *Cultural Studies*, (23), 2014,
221-235. (藤井 千冬.「ハックの「自然」と「文 明」:「自由」からみる理想
的な社会」.『文化学研究』(23), 2014, 221-235.)

Greeson, Michael P. "Hobbes, Locke, and the State of Nature
Theories: A Reassessment." *Episteme* 5.1 (1994): 2.

Gueusquin, Marie-France. *Le Mois des Dragons*. Bibliothèque
    Berger-Levrault, 1981. グースカン, マリ＝フランス.『フランスの祭りと暦──
    五月の女王とドラゴン』樋口淳訳.原書房, 1991年

Hamamoto, Ryuzo. "The Origins of Relativization." *Journal of Mark
    Twain Studies*, Issue No. 15. Nan'un-do, 2016. (浜本隆三.「相対
    化の源流」.『マーク・トウェイン研究と批評 第15号』.南雲堂, 2016.)

Hatano, Masaru. *Interestingly Well understood! The Book of
    Philosophy.* Seitosha, 2012. (秦野勝.『面白いほどよくわかる！ 哲学の
    本』. 西東社, 2012年.)

Hayashi, Nobuhiro. *Reading Emile*. Law Bunka Sha, 1987. 林信弘.
    『「エミール」を読む』.法律文化社, 1987年.

Higashi, Yoshiro. "Mark Twain and Nature: An Interpretation of *The
    Adventures of Huckleberry Finn*. Literature and Economics."
    Literature and Economics. (1), 1980, 13-34. 東義郎.「Mark
    Twainと自然──The Adventures of Huckleberry Finn の一解釈
    ─」.『文経論叢. 文学科篇』. (1), 1980, 13-34.

Honjo, Seiji. "*The Adventures of Huckleberry Finn*: A Study of
    Nature and Mark Twain's Autonomy." *Mukogawa Women's
    University Bulletin*, Faculty of Literature. (本城精二.「*The
    Adventures of Huckleberry Finn* 研究 ─自然の描写と Mark Twain
    の自由観」.『武庫川女子大学紀要 文学部編』. (34), 1986, 55-69.)

Ishihara, Tsuyoshi. "Tom Sawyer and Huck Finn as Read by Children under Occupation." *Journal of Mark Twain Studies*, Issue No. 6. Nan'un-do, 2007. (石原剛.「占領下の子どもたちが読んだ『トム・ソーヤ』と『ハック・フィン』.『マーク・トウェイン研究と批評 第6号』. 南雲堂, 2007.)

Issitt, Micah, and Carlyn Main. *Hidden Religion: The Greatest Mysteries and Symbols of the World's Religious Beliefs.* ABC-CLIO, 2014.

Igawa, Masago. "A Journey into the Colonies of the Empire." *Journal of Mark Twain Studies*, Issue No. 4. Nan'un-do, 2005. (井川眞砂.「大帝国植民地への旅」.『マーク・トウェイン研究と批評 第4号』. 南雲堂, 2005.)

---. "Sam Clemens's Hannibal." *Journal of Mark Twain Studies*, Issue No. 7. Nan'un-do, 2008. ---. (井川眞砂.「サム・クレメンズのハンニバル」.『マーク・トウェイン研究と批評 第7号』.

南雲堂, 2008年.)

---. "Mark Twain's Literary 'Historical' Legacy." *Journal of Mark Twain Studies*, Issue No. 10. Nan'un-do, 2011.

Ido, Keiko. "Nature in American Literature: Huckleberry and Gatsby's Pursuit of Dreams." *Journal of Komazawa Women's University.* (12), 2005, 15-23. (井戸 桂子.「アメリカ文学における自然—ハックルベリーとギャツビーの追い求める夢」『駒沢女子大学研究紀要』.

(12), 2005, 15-23.)

Inoue, Hirotsugu. H. D. "Thoreau's Ethical View." *Eiji Daigaku Ronso*
    (45), 2011, 35-55. (井上 博嗣.「H・D・ソローの倫理観」.『英知大学論
    叢』. (45), 2011, 35-55.)

LeMaster, J.R, and Wilson, James. eds., *The Mark Twain
    Encyclopedia*. Garland P,1993.

Ishihara, Tsuyoshi. "Mark Twain's Literary Historical Legacy: Tracing
    four literary histories." *Journal of Mark Twain Studies*. Issue
    No.10. Nan'un-do, 2011.『マーク・トウェインの文学「史」的遺産』.『マー
    ク・トウェイン研究と批評 第10号』, 南雲堂, 2011年.

Jonge, Francien, Bos & Ruud van den, eds. *The Human-animal
    Relationship*: *Forever and a Day*. Royal Van Gorcum, 2005.

Kamei, Shunsuke. *The World of Mark Twain*, Nan'un-do, 1995. 亀井
    俊介.『マーク・トウェインの世界』南雲堂, 1995年.)

---. *Huck Finn's Amerca*, Chuokoron-Shinsha. (亀井俊介.『ハックルベリー・
    フィンのアメリカ：「自由」はどこにあるか』. 中央公論新社, 2009年.)

Kambara, Masaaki. "The Legend of Wild Man: Transformation of
    Images in the Late Middle Ages (1)." *Bulletin of Kurashiki
    University of Arts and Sciences* (10), 2005, 3-13. (神原 正明.
    「ワイルド・マン伝説--中世末期におけるイメージの変容(1)」『倉敷芸術科学
    大学紀要』. (10), 2005, 3-13.)

---. "The Legend of Wild Man: Transformation of Images in the Late Middle Ages (2)." *Bulletin of Kurashiki University of Arts and Sciences* (11), 2006, 3-14. (神原 正明.「ワイルドマン伝説--中世末期におけるイメージの変容(2)」『倉敷芸術科学大学紀要』. (11), 2006, 3-14.)

---. "The Legend of Wild Man: Transformation of Images in the Late Middle Ages (3)." *Bulletin of Kurashiki University of Arts and Sciences* (12), 2007, 3-14. (神原 正明.「ワイルドマン伝説--中世末期におけるイメージの変容(3)」『倉敷芸術科学大学紀要』. (12), 2007, 3-14.)

---. "The Legend of Wild Man: Transformation of Images in the Late Middle Ages (4)." *Bulletin of Kurashiki University of Arts and Sciences*. (13), 2008, 3-14. (神原 正明.「ワイルドマン伝説--中世末期におけるイメージの変容(4)」『倉敷芸術科学大学紀要』. (13), 2008, 3-14.)

Kamiya, Naoki. *Minnano Center Textbook of Ethics*. Obunsha, 2015. (神谷直樹. (『みんなのセンター教科書倫理』. 旺文社, 2015年.)

Kawamoto, Toru. "The Stagecoach to the American West." *Journal of Mark Twain Studies*, Issue No. 15. Nan'un-do, 2016. (川本徹.「アメリカン・ウエスト行きの駅馬車」.『マーク・トウェイン研究と批評第15号』. 南雲堂, 2016年.)

Kokubun, Koichiro. *Modern Political Philosophy*. Chikuma Shobo, 2015. (國分功一郎.『近代政治哲学』. 筑摩書房, 2015年)

Kolb, Harold H. *Mark Twain: The Gift of Humor.* UP of America, 2015.

Konstam, Angus. *The History of Pirates.* Mercury Books, 2005.

Kucich, John J. *Ghostly Communion: Cross-Cultural Spiritualism in Nineteenth-Century American Literature.* UP of New Hampshire, 2004.

Loving, Jerome. *Mark Twain: The Adventures of Samuel L. Clemens.* U of California P, 2011.

McIntire-Strasburg, Janice. "Mark Twain in Vienna: A Diplomat without Pay." *Cosmopolitan Twain.* Eds. Ann, Ryan and McCullough, Joseph. U of Missouri P, 2008.

Maeyashiki, Taro. "Mark Twain's Image of African Americans--Jim as a 'natural man' in *Adventures of Huckleberry Finn.*" U of Kitakyushu, Master's Thesis.

Maik, Thomas. "Personal Recollections of Joan of Arc (1886)." *The Mark Twain Encyclopedia* Eds. LeMaster, J.R, and Wilson, James. Garland P, 1993.

Marlowe, Frank. *The Hadza: Hunter-gatherers of Tanzania.* U of California P, 2010.

Masui, Shizuyo. "Mark Twain and the Age of Evangelicalism." *Journal of Mark Twain Studies*, Issue No. 8. Nan'un-do, 2009. (増井志津代.「マーク・トウェインと福音主義の時代」.『マーク・トウェイン研究と批評 第8号』. 南雲堂, 2009.)

Matsumura, Akira, ed. *Daijirin* (Major Dictionary), 2nd Edition. Sanseido, 1995. 松村明編.『大辞林』第2版. 三省堂, 1995年.

McKay, Janet, H. "'An Art So High: Style in the *Adventures of Huckleberry Finn*," *New Essays on Adventures of Huckleberry Finn* Ed. Louis Budd. Cambridge UP, 1985.

Misugi, Keiko. "Twain and Dos Passos's Critique of War." *Journal of Mark Twain Studies*, Issue No. 13. Nan'un-do, 2014. (三杉圭子.「トウェインとドス・パソスの戦争批判」.『マーク・トウェイン研究と批評第13号』. 南雲堂, 2014)

Michelet, Jules, and Wight, Orlando Williams. *Joan of Arc: Or, The Maid of Orleans*. United States, n.p, 1858.

Meltzer, Milton. *Mark Twain Himself: A Pictorial Biography*. U of Missouri P, 2002.

Morris, Linda M. *Gender Play in Mark Twain: Cross Dressing and Transgression.* U of Missouri P 2007.

Mounce, William D. *Why I Trust the Bible: Answers to Real Questions and Doubts People Have about the Bible*. Zondervan Reflective, 2021.

Murray, Margaret. *The God of the Witches*. Oxford UP, 1931.『魔女の
　　神』.西村稔訳. 人文書院, 1995.

---. *Life As I Find It: A Treasury of Mark Twain Rarities*. Cooper
　　Square P, 1961.

Nakajima, Yoshinobu. "Mark Twain and American Nationalism:
　　Indian Images in *Roughing It*." *Bulletin of Shiraume Gakuen
　　Junior College*, (31), 1995, 51-58. (中島好伸.「マーク・トウェインとア
　　メリカのナショナリズム : *Roughing It*におけるインディアン像」.『白梅学園短
　　期大学紀要』. (31), 1995, 51-58.)

Narváez, Darcia et al. eds. *Ancestral Landscapes in Human
　　Evolution: Culture, Childrearing and Social Wellbeing*. Oxford
　　UP, 2014.

Netton, Ian, R. Islam. *Christianity and the Mystic Journey: A
　　Comparative Exploration*. Edinburgh UP, 2011.

Okin, Susan M. *Women in Western Political Thought*. Princeton UP,
　　1979. オーキン, スーザン.『政治思想のなかの女』.田林葉, 重森臣広訳.晃
　　洋書房, 2010年.

Pettit, Arthur, G. *Mark Twain & South*. UP of Kentucky, 1974.

Pickett, Joseph P., et al. *The American Heritage Dictionary of the
　　English Language*. Houghton Mifflin Harcourt, 2018.

Philpot, J. H. *The Sacred Tree in Religion and Myth*. Mineola: Dover
　　Publications, 2004.

Phipps, William E. *Mark Twain's Religion*. Mercer UP, 2003.

Qvortrup, Mads. *The Political Philosophy of Jean-Jacques Rousseau the Impossibility of Reason*. Manchester P, 2003.

Rainey, Betty F. *The Representation of Satan in the Fiction of Samuel L. Clemens*. MA thesis, North Texas State University, 1971.

Railton, Stephen. *Mark Twain: A Short Introduction*. Blackwell, 2004.

Rasmussen, R. Kent, and John H. Davis. *Critical Companion to Mark Twain: A Literary Reference to His Life and Work*. Facts On File, 2007.

Rieder, John, and Larry E. Smith. *Multiculturalism and Representation: Selected Essays*. College of Languages, Linguistics, and Literature, Univ. of Hawaii, 1996.

Rousseau, Jean-Jacques. *Emile*. trans. Allan Bloom. New York: Basic Books, 2005.

---. *Confessions*. Wordsworth Editions Limited, 1996.

---. *Émile: Ou, De L'éducation*. Ulan P, 2005.

---.*On the Origin of Inequality*. Cosimo Classics, 2005.

---. *Discours sur l'Origine et les Fondements de l'Inégalité parmi les Hommes*. Paris: Bibliothèque Nationale, 1884.

---. *On the Origin of Inequality*. trans. Gen Nakayama, Koubunsha, 2008. (ルソー, ジャン＝ジャック.『人間不平等起源論』. 中山元訳. 光文社, 2008.)

---. *Essay on the Original Language and Writings Related to Music*. UP of New England, 1988.

---. Trans. John Scott T. *Essay on the Origin of Languages and Writings Related to Music*. Hanover: UP of England, 1998.

---. *On Philosophy, Morality, and Religion*. ed. Kelly Christopher. Dartmouth College P, 2007.

---. *The Social Contract & Discourse*. Devoted Publishing, 2016.

Rowe, John Carlos. *Literary Culture and U.S. Imperialism from the Revolution to World War II*. Oxford UP, 2000.

Ruth, Siebert C. *Huckleberry Finn by Mark Twain (MAXnotes)*. Research and Education Association,1994.

Sano, Morio. *The Mythical World of Huck and Tom*. Sairyusha, 1996. (佐野守男.『ハックとトムの神話世界』. 彩流社,1996.)

Satouchi, Katsumi. "Freedom and Servitude: Dickens and Twain's Representations of Slavery." *Journal of Mark Twain Studies*, Issue No. 14. Nan'un-do, 2015. 里内克巳.「自由と隷属：ディケンズとトウェインの奴隷制表象」.『マーク・トウェイン研究と批評 第14号』. 南雲堂, 2015年.)

Satouchi, Katsumi. *Which Was It?*, Sairyusha, 2015. (里内克訳.「『それ
　　はどっちだったか』. 彩流社, 2015年.」)

Scharnhorst. ed. *Mark Twain: The Complete Interviews*. The U of
　　Alabama P, 2006.

Schultz, Jeffrey D. ed. *Encyclopedia of Minorities in American
　　Politics: Hispanic Americans and Native Americans*. The Oryx P,
　　2000.

Scott, John T. *Jean-Jacques Rousseau: Human Nature and History*.
　　Routledge, 2006.

Serafin, Steven ed. *The Continuum Encyclopedia of American
　　Literature*. Continuum P Group Inc,. 2003.

Shibuya, Akira. "Mark Twain as a Fantasy Writer." *Journal of Mark
　　Twain Studies*, Issue No. 3. Nan'un-do, 2004. (渋谷章.「ファンタジ
　　ー作家としてのマーク・トウェイン」.『マーク・トウェイン研究と批評 第3号』. 南雲
　　堂, 2004年.)

Stone, Albert , E. "Joan of Arc" *On Mark Twain*. ed Louis J. Budd,
　　Duke UP, 1987.

Stoneley, Peter. *Mark Twain and the Feminine Aesthetic*. Cambridge
　　UP, 1992.

Strauss, Leo. *Natural Right and History*. U of Chicago P, 1953.

Sugiyama, Naoto. "The Flood of the River and the Novelist's Imagination." *Journal of Mark Twain Studies*, Issue No. 1. Nan'un-do, 2002. (杉山直人.「河の氾濫と小説家の想像力」.『マーク・トウェイン研究と批評 第1号』. 南雲堂, 2002年.)

Sugizaki, Taiichiro. *Hyakki Yakosho: Fantasy and Idealism in Medieval Europe.* Hara Shobo, 2002. (杉崎泰一郎.『欧州百鬼夜行抄：幻想と理想のはざまの中世ヨーロッパ』. 原書房, 2002年.)

Suzuki, Keisuke. "Black Representation in Adventures of Huckleberry Finn." *Kanagawa University Graduate School of Language and Culture* (22), 2016.31-72. (鈴木 惠介.「『ハックルベリー・フィンの冒険』における黒人表象」『神奈川大学大学院言語と文化論集』(22), 2016.31-72.)

Taga Keiji. *Medieval Performing Arts: East and West.* Bungeisha, 2000. 多賀敬二. (『中世上演芸術・東と西』. 文芸社, 2000年.)

Takayama Kazuhiko. *Jeanne d'Arc: A "saint" who continues to live on in history.* (高山一彦 『ジャンヌ・ダルク: 歴史を生き続ける「聖女」』岩波新書, 2005年.)

Takeda, Takako. "The Formation of the Twain Brand." *Journal of Mark Twain Studies,* Issue No. 15. Nan'un-do, 2016. (武田貴子.「トウェイン・ブランドの成立」.『マーク・トウェイン研究と批評 第15号』. 南雲堂, 2016年.)

Tabei, Kouji "From White to Red: Twain and the American Indian."
Whiteness and American Literature, Kaibunsha, 2016. (田部井
考次.「白から赤へ―トウェインとアメリカ・インディアン」.『ホワイトネスとアメリカ文
学』. 開文社, 2016年.

The American Heritage Dictionary of the English Language (5th
edition). Houghton Mifflin, 2000.

The New Georgia Guide. U of Georgia P, 1996.

Tomita, Naohisa. "I wonder if Twain saw Strange Dreams?" *Journal
of Mark Twain Studies*, Issue No. 1. Nan'un-do, 2002. (富田直
久.「トウェインは「奇妙な夢」を観たのだろうか？」.『マーク・トウェイン研究と批
評 第1号』. 南雲堂, 2002年.)

Tomlinson, David, O. "Calvinism." *The Mark Twain Encyclopedia*. Ed.
J.R. LeMaster. Garland P, 1993.

Trites, Roberta S. *Twain, Alcott, and the Birth of the Adolescent
Reform Novel*. U of Iowa P, 2007.

Tsuji, Kazuhiko. "Twain's Dreams." *Journal of Mark Twain Studies*,
Issue No. 1. Nankumodo, 2002. (辻和彦.「双生の夢」.『マーク・トウェ
イン研究と批評 第1号』. 南雲堂, 2002年.

---. "Mark Twain's View of Nature in Huck and Tom Among the
Indians." *The Literary and Environmental Studies Association*,
(2), 5-11, 1999. (辻和彦.「インディアンの中のハックとトム」におけるマーク・
トウェインの自然観」『文学・環境学会』(2), 5-11, 1999.)

Tsujimoto, Yoko. "The Two-Lane Detective Reconsidered." *Journal of Mark Twain Studies*, Issue No. 2. Nan'un-do, 2003.「辻本庸子.「二連式探偵再考」.『マーク・トウェイン研究と批評 第2号』. 南雲堂, 2003年」

Tuckey, Janet. *Joan of Arc: The Maid*. G.P. Putnam's Sons, 1890.

Twain, Mark. *Adventures of Huckleberry Finn*. New York: Norton, 1999.

---. *The Autobiography of Mark Twain*. Ed. Charles Neider. Harper & Brothers, 1959.

---. *Autobiography of Mark Twain. volume 1*. eds. Smith *et al*. U of California P, 2010.

---. *Autobiography of Mark Twain. volume 2*. eds, Griffin, Benjamin, Harriet Smith, E.U of California P, 2010.

---. *Autobiography of Mark Twain, Volume 3*. eds. Benjamin Griffin *et al*. Oakland: U of California P, 2015.

---. *The Annotated Huckleberry Finn*. ed. Michael Patrick Hearn. Norton, 1981.

---. *The Adventures of Tom Sawyer*. Norton, 2007.

---. *Huck Finn and Tom Sawyer among the Indians*. Los Angeles: U of California P, 1938.

---. *Letters from the Earth*. Harper & Row Publisher, 1962.

---. *Life on the Mississippi*. Dover Publications, 2000.

---. *The Mysterious Stranger Manuscript*. ed. William Gibson. U of California P, 2005.

---. Mark Twain: *Collected Tales, Sketches, Speeches, and Essays, Volume 2:1891-1910*. ed. Robert H. Hirst. Library of America, 1992.

---. "Captain Stormfield's Visit to Heaven." *The Bible According to Mark Twain*. Eds. Howard G. Baetzhold *et al*. U of Georgia P, 1995.

---. *Personal Recollections of Joan of Arc*. Leonaur, 2011.

---. *Roughing it*. American Publishing Company, 1872.

---. "Which was the Dream?" *The Devil's Race-track: Mark Twain's Great Dark Writings*. U of

California P, 1966.

---. *Following the Equator*. Harper Collins P, 1897.

---. *Personal Recollections of Joan of Arc*. Leonaur, 2011.

Twain, Mark, and Charles Neider. "Extract from Captain Stormfield's Visit to Heaven." *The Complete Short Stories of Mark Twain*. Bantam Books, 2005.

Twain, Mark, et al. *The Letters of Mark Twain*. 1st World Library Literary Society, 2005.

Twain, Mark, and John Sutton Tuckey. *Mark Twain's Which Was the Dream and Other Symbolic Writings of the Later Years*. U of California P, 1967.

Tucker, Spencer C. ed. *The Encyclopedia of North American Indian Wars, 1607-1890: A Political, Social, and Military History* [3 volumes]. ABC-CLIO,LLC, 2011.

Uzawa, Yoshiko. "Literature, Advertising, and Capitalism." *Journal of Mark Twain Studies*, Issue No. 9. Nan'un-do, 2010. (宇沢美子.「文学・広告・資本主義」.『マーク・トウェイン研究と批評 第9号』. 南雲堂, 2010年。

Uenishi Tetsuo. "Frontiers of Religion." *Journal of Mark Twain Studies*, Issue No. 8. Nan'un-do, 2009. 上西哲雄.「宗教のフロンティア」.『マーク・トウェイン研究と批評 第8号』. 南雲堂, 2009年.

Varner, Gary R. *The Mythic Forest, the Green Man and the Spirit of Nature*. Algora P, 2006.

Velm ,Greg. *Wiley AP U.S. History*. Hoboken: John Wiley & Sons, Inc. 2013.

Waguri, Ryo. "Does Twain Affirm Joan of Arc?" *Journal of Mark Twain Studies*, Issue No. 13. Nan'un-do, 2014. (和栗了.「トウェインはジャンヌ・ダルクを肯定しているのか？」.『マーク・トウェイン研究と批評 第13号』. 南雲堂, 2014年.)

Watanabe, Toshio. "Genius is not enough." *Journal of Mark Twain Studies*, Issue No. 11. Nan'un-do, 2012. (渡辺利雄. "Genius is not enough".『マーク・トウェイン研究と批評 第11号』. 南雲堂, 2012年.)

Watson, Ronald Ross. *Nutrition and AIDS, Second Edition*. Boca Raton: CRC P, 2001.

Weisenburger, Steven C. *A Gravity's Rainbow Companion: Sources and Contexts for Pynchon's Novel*. A U of Georgia P, 2006.

Wilson, James. *The Mark Twain Encyclopedia* Eds. in LeMaster, J.R, and Wilson, James. eds., . Garland P, 1993.

Woodburn, James. "An Introduction to Hadza Ecology." *Man the Hunter*. eds. Richard Barry and Lee De Vore *et al*. Adline Transaction P, 2009.

Wright, R. Terry. *The Genesis of fiction: Modern Novelists as Biblical interpreters*. Routledge, 2007.

Yamamoto, Yuko. *Mark Twain's Unfinished Works: Huck Finn and Tom Sawyer Among the Indians. A Journey into Memory and Deep Psychology. English Literature Reading through Memory*. Kaibunsha, 2013. (山本裕子.「マーク・トウェインの未完作品—インディアンの中のハック・フィンとトム・ソーヤ: 記憶と深層心理を探る旅」.『＜記憶＞で読む英語文学』.開文社, 2013年.)

Yokoyama, Hideki. "On *Adventures of Huckleberry* Finn: A Journey
    Lost in Natural Forces." *Ashikaga Institute of Technology
    Research Collection*, (16) 1990, 223-230. (横山秀樹.「『ハックルベ
    リー・フィンの冒険』について— 自然力に迷妄する旅の行方」『足利工業大学
    研究集録』(16)1990, 223-230.)

Youngblood, Wayne. *Mark Twain along the Mississippi*. World
    Almanac Library, 2006.

Zuckert, Catherine H. *Natural Right and the American Imagination:
    Political Philosophy in Novel Form*. Rowman & Littlefield P,
    2009.